CEREMON

An introductory guide, by a
the mechanisms of ceremon
of the Gol

CW00816059

CEREMONIAL MAGIC
A GUIDE TO THE MECHANISMS OF RITUAL

BY

ISRAEL REGARDIE

AEON

Published 2007
by Aeon Books
www.aeonbooks.co.uk

British Library Cataloguing in Publication Data
A C.I.P. is available for this book from the British Library

ISBN 9781904658108

Printed and bound in Great Britain

Contents

PART ONE

CHAPTER I

Basic Principles

It may be asked for what purpose this book has been written. Why should one bother with ceremonial magic of this type? The question is valid. But in view of the fact that so much has been written in recent years about magic itself, the answer should be so clearly apparent to any student of the subject that I do not feel disposed to cope with it here and now at any length.

One may mention first of all *The Mystical Qabalah* of Dion Fortune, which provides the theoretical basis of ritual magic. Then there are the several books of W. E. Butler, all on the same topic, excellent texts for the student to study for a long time. William Gray's *Ladder of Lights* is a masterpiece to be put in a similar catagory with the book by Dion Fortune mentioned above. Gareth Knight has written a fine little book *The Practice of Ritual Magic*. Certainly the writings of Aleister Crowley on this topic must never be neglected; he is the primary expositor on this subject in modern times. *Gems From the Equinox* as well as his *Magick in Theory and Practice* will give the student a good deal of material which may take years to assimilate and to use properly.

A couple of my own books may be consulted to considerable advantage. *The Golden Dawn* is a *must*; I can say this without any sense of egotism for I was only the editor, not the author of the material contained in those (original) four volumes. *The Tree of Life* may help to clarify and coordinate a great deal of the apparently disconnected material of both Crowley and the The Golden Dawn. Finally, *Foundations of Practical Magic* (Aquarian Press, 1979) should be mentioned as a general introduction to the whole practical side of the subject. With this material assimilated, what follows in this book should not be too mysterious, nor the motives for practising it.

What is to be gained from the frequent, or, even better, the daily repetition of this ritual is at the very least an enormous increase in psycho-spiritual sensitivity. The student who has spent some time on the basic disciplines described in *Twelve Steps to Spiritual Enlightenment*, or some other similar regimen, will find himself in a position to obtain a very great deal more from the ritual than the student approaching this without due preparation.

Despite the fact that illumination is in effect a sudden and immediate event, it is nonetheless equally true that enhancing the sensitivity of the organism may well prepare the way for such an event to occur. There are no absolute rules laid down anywhere that guarantee enlightenment. 'The spirit bloweth where it listeth.' No man is in a position to say who, or when, or why any one individual is subject to this descent of the holy spirit.

The fact remains, however, that most systems of initiation are predicated on preparing the organism for this most precious experience. There is to be a refining of the elemental vehicles through which the Self may function, an equilibration of the total organism so that when enlightenment does occur, the stresses and strains to which the organism may be subject will not disrupt its natural and integrated functions. Insanity is not one of the goals of spiritual growth and development – although it occurs far too often to make one feel comfortable when contemplating the present occult scene. Proper preparation, self-discipline and daily practice are still the time-honoured approaches to the gateway of the higher mysteries and character-transformation.

One of the more effective traditional methods of preparing a room for use as a temple for active ritual work or for quiet meditation, is called 'Opening by Watch Tower'. It may seem to the beginner frightfully complex and difficult. In reality, however, when studied, and above all when practised, it becomes remarkably simple and direct. Besides possessing its own utility as well as charm, the method is capable of development in a variety of different directions so that, if need be, it can be elaborated into a major ritual for all occasions and all purposes. It may require some study first, followed by some little practical experience over a period of weeks or months – depending on personal ability, as well as time available – before this conclusion may be recognized.

It incorporates most of the better features that once characterized the Golden Dawn. These include the Pentagram and Hexagram Rituals, which need to be studied and meditated upon. In a special sense, the Pentagram is another ritual which, with deliberation, can become a complete ceremony in its own right. It includes a complete armamentarium of approaches which the casual student may not perceive at first sight.

The term 'Watch-Towers' is borrowed from the Enochian system of Dr John Dee and Edward Kelley. They theorized that at each quarter of the earth stood a tower guarded by angelic and elemental forces. These metaphysical concepts are represented in actual practice by the Elemental Tablets placed at the four points of the compass in the temple or room being used.

The full comprehension of these Tablets demands close attention to and study of the Enochian Section of Vol. IV of *The Golden Dawn*. Admittedly, to draw and paint the Tablets requires the expenditure of much time and energy, and this might make some students hesitate before going any further. However, a compromise is available, lessening the demand for time and energy. The sigils at the top of each Tablet or Watchtower may be painted on board – or any other material the student desires to use – having the arbitrary dimensions of about six inches by six inches.

These sigils from *The Golden Dawn*, which gives the colours, etc., to be used in their construction, are reproduced in Vol. IV of *The Golden Dawn*. Pastels or crayons or coloured paper may be used. If one has skill enough, oil or acrylic paints may be used, but these can be messy unless the student has previously acquired experience with them. I am partial to the use of poster colours on Bristol board, spraying them with clear lacquer a day or so after they have achieved full drying. These should be hung or pinned on the wall in the appropriate quarter.

I do not suggest that the student plunges headlong into the working of this ritual. There need be no hurry. What is required is some familiarization with the contents of the ritual so that the on-going movement may be perceived. Then a few trial runs, as it were, may be attempted just to get the feel. With these trial runs, some of the ritual wording may be memorized. This should not provide much difficulty. I suggest working with the written text in front of one for some little time, in which case memorization will occur by rote and without strain or effort.

This book is divided into sections showing how the ritual is built up from scratch. There is also an Appendix which gives the Pentagram and Hexagram Rituals and other pertinent material. These should be memorized so that full attention can be given thereafter to the Watchtower Ritual itself. This is another reason why the student should not hasten to arrive at the end immediately.

Incidentally, I am using the word 'student' throughout. We are all students, and should be forever. There is so much to learn and apply. Words such as 'magus', or 'adeptus minor', or other such grandiloquent titles, have been deliberately omitted in favour of this simple word 'student'. All of us are in this one simple category.

The ritual itself is first presented in all its simplicity. Study it well. Then in a succeeding section, additions will be made. These additions are extrapolated from the elemental Grades of the Order of the Golden Dawn and from Vol. I, No. 8 *Equinox*. Note them well, please. In these grades, the officiating officer invokes the Elements by a specific process so that they may influence the aura and character of the candidate undergoing initiation. This specific process is added in the appropriate place to the Watchtower Ritual, lengthening it a little bit, but rendering it not only more explicit to the student, but more potent. It would not be amiss, then, to read into this statement that the Watchtower Ritual may be turned into a ritual of self-initiation.

I would like to remind the reader that this study has made no mention deliberately of some of the basic psycho-spiritual techniques operative in ceremonial magic. The assumption of God-forms at the appropriate quarters, the method of vibration of divine and angelic names, and the use of spirit-vision are some of the major methods to be used with a rubric of this kind. I have omitted them, however, in order to keep this study as simple as possible. When the student becomes more adept in using this form of ritual, he may gradually add to his armamentarium these other devices which are fully described in other textbooks, notably *The Middle Pillar*. Though this book is now considerably outdated and will be rewritten in the near future, it is still a useful book of instruction.

One of the reasons for starting off the ceremony with the Pentagram Ritual is not only to clear a space for the working, but to insure that the entire operation is under the aegis of the Higher Self. This is one of the major characteristics of the Golden Dawn outlook. In one of the higher grades, a clause in the Oath is to the effect that in each operation of magic the student pledges to work under and to employ only the highest divine names that he knows. 'For by names and images are all powers awakened and re-awakened.'

A later section then reproduces the Prayers of the Elements that are given at the close of each of the elemental grades. These are long beautiful prayers expressing the aspirations and nature of each elemental kingdom. Each prayer may be used *in toto* in the appropriate place; these will be clearly indicated. They are long, it is true, but they impart much beauty and power to the ritual. If too long for the average student, they may well be abbreviated.

For many months, in the mid-thirties, I used a variation of this ritual with about a half-dozen sentences extrapolated from each prayer. They picked up the essence of the longer prayer and served my purpose very well. Each student might attempt this on his own behalf if he finds using each prayer lengthens the ritual too much.

Finally, there is another section which uses one of the Golden Dawn invocations from the 5=6 Ritual, together with the closing paragraph of the so-called Bornless Ritual. Contrary to some recently expressed opinions, this was *never* an official ritual of the Order. Not that it matters very much. It has a quality of its own, adding a species of fervour and intensity to the ritual which converts it into an Invocation of the Higher Self, or the Holy Guardian Angel, so-called.

Crowley, at various periods of his life, seemed forever unable to decide whether the Holy Guardian Angel or the Higher and Divine Genius of The Golden Dawn was the same as the Higher Self, or an Angelic being totally independent of man. The bulk of his writing however tends to identify them – the Higher Self *is* the Holy

Guardian Angel. This is more or less confirmed, if we need confirmation, by Blavatsky's remark in *The Secret Doctrine* that 'The Watcher, or the divine prototype, is at the upper rung of the ladder of being; the shadow at the lower. Withal, the *Monad* of every living being ... *is an individual Dhyan Chohan (god), distinct from others, a kind of spiritual individuality of its own*, during one special Manvantara.' This is further confirmed by Mathers in his profound essay 'On Man, the Microcosm' in Vol. I of *The Golden Dawn* in which he relates the Higher Self to the Divine Genius as an Angel, part of an ever-ascending hierarchy of spiritual beings.

> The Shining Flame of the Divine Fire, the *Kether* of the Body, is the Real Self of the Incarnation ... This *Yechidah* is the only part of the man which can truly say – EHEIEH, I am. This is then but the Kether of the Assiah of the Microcosm, that is, it is the highest part of man as Man ... Behind *Yechidah* are Angelic and Archangelic Forces of which *Yechidah* is the manifestor. It is therefore the Lower Genius or Viceroy of the Higher Genius which is beyond, an Angel Mighty and Terrible. This Great Angel is the higher Genius, beyond which are the Archangelic and Divine.

This, in effect, completes the study of the ritual, beginning with its use as simply a means of preparing a room for use as a temple and winding up with an invocation of the Higher Self.

One writer recently ridiculed me indirectly by deriding the idea that in working a ritual a good 'head of steam' has to be generated. I would like to remind him, and others of the same ilk, that an example of *good* ritual, from a technical point of view, is to be found in the Masonic Order. I doubt if there is to be found anywhere else in the world comparable accoutrements, environment, training, etc. They are very impressive to watch. Any Mason will confirm this – without betraying any of the secrets he is bound to withhold from the non-Mason. In my teens I was a member of the Order of De Molay, a junior Masonic organization, started by Masons, superintended by Masons, and, in effect, conducted by Masons. It had the same beautiful paraphernalia, the same superb coaching to produce the right stage effect, the same kind of pomp, order and stateliness. In a word, its rituals are copies of Masonic rituals without the traditional Masonic mystery. If this is my critic's idea of good magical ritual, I can only assure him that he is way off. They are stately and very impressive, without doubt, but they are far from magical, no matter how well the officiants have learned their lines nor how smoothly or effectively the team may operate. Nothing is achieved on a magical level.

Working correctly with ritual has to evoke a species of inner excitation, more than merely a mood, which exalts the mind to reach upwards to its own divine root. A cold, stately, perfectly executed rite will never achieve this, no matter how clear and accurate the visualizations, etc., may be.

A few words are necessary about equipment and paraphernalia. These are matters to which the beginner usually bestows undue attention, using them unconsciously as devices to deter him from beginning any magical work whatsoever. It seems too appallingly difficult to get everything together – a room with privacy, the symbols upon the altar, and the so-called elemental weapons. When reading the instructions preceding magical rituals, there seem to be so many requisites that are practically beyond him at this stage of development as to cause him to lose heart and interest.

I would like to insist that so many of these can be simplified down to the point where even the novice can comply without complicating his life and his intellectual capabilities to any major degree. For example: the altar can be almost any small table about waist-high. Spread on it a black cloth – black, because it is neutral; some other colour would attract one's attention unnecessarily. The basic symbols to be placed on it are those of the Golden Dawn – the red cross and the white triangle. Surely it is not difficult to cut from white pasteboard a white equilateral triangle with a base of two or three inches?

The cross does not necessarily carry with it a Christian significance. In Volume I of *The Golden Dawn*, the knowledge lectures ascribe different meaning to the several forms of the cross. For our purpose here, however, it is the equal-armed cross that is used and represents equilibrium and a balanced disposition of whatever elements are involved.

The cross should be equal-armed (actually comprised of five

squares) about three inches high or wide and painted red. The cross
should be placed above the white triangle, towards the middle of
the altar. Now that is not very difficult, is it?

So far as the instruments are concerned: if you have made them,
well and good. Full instructions have been given in *The Golden
Dawn* that are not too difficult to comply with. The Watchtower
Ritual actually will comprise a sort of consecration ceremony if you
have made them. If not, it does not matter. At the East, on the altar,
place a small fan made from a sheet of typing paper that you have
carefully folded, as any child will show you, to represent the
element of Air. In the South, for the element of Fire, use an incense
stick; or if you do not have any, just place a small unused book of
matches in the right place. In the West, to represent Water, a small
glass of water. While in the North, a few crumbs of bread and a few
grains of salt may be placed on a tiny saucer or platter to represent
Earth. It is just as simple as that. For the element of Spirit, place a
freshly cut flower, a rose or whatever else is in season, on top of the
triangle and cross in the centre of the altar. This completely solves
the whole complex problem of instruments and so forth.

Robes, special clothing, collars, breast-plates and lamens, all of
these considerations may be left alone until such time as the student
feels ready to undertake their manufacture and use. Washing or
bathing before the ceremony may be enough at the outset. After he
has studied the subject sufficiently intensively from the textbooks
where these topics are dealt with, then he may feel sufficiently
secure to attempt their use. On the other hand, if he fares well in the
ceremony, he may feel no need to complicate matters by the use of
technical paraphernalia and equipment.

When the proper time arrives for coping with such details, the
books already mentioned will provide the necessary information.
However, Robert Wang has recently compiled a book based on *The
Golden Dawn* and some verbal information from me that should fill
the bill even better. It is entitled *The Secret Temple* (Samuel Weiser,
1980). It takes the basic Golden Dawn material and expands it from
the point of view of the practically-minded student who wants to
equip his temple properly and by his own efforts. Full and detailed
instruction is given on the manufacture of the elemental and other

weapons, banners of the East and West, Pillars of the Temple, the altar, robes, and many other similar matters.

But again, let me insist, leave all of this detail severely alone until you have acquired some expertise with ceremonial work, and feel the need for more adequate and complete material to work with.

It would be ideal if you had a room which you could reserve only for meditation and magical working. Today, however, with more people living in apartments than ever before, and space being so very limited, this may be impossible. If it is impossible, use whatever room is available – the bedroom, the living room, the den, or whatever. You should be assured of temporary privacy; that at least is an essential, so have a lock or bolt on this door. Or request those you live with not to enter your room at certain hours when you are working.

All problems relating to the mere technicalities of ritual procedure should be solved in the same way, simply and easily and directly. This is why some preliminary study and meditation is required, so that you know what you are doing and why. Do not do things blindly, merely because a book tells you to. Understand the reasons for what you do and what you employ. They are basically simple and the existing literature, in spite of some complicating features, really does explain the fundamentals. Mystification has no part in magic. Simplicity and sincerity and enthusiasm have.

CHAPTER II

Ritual of Opening by Watchtower

1. *Stand at Altar, facing East, announce:*

HEKAS, HEKAS, ESTE BEBELOI!
(hay-kahs, hay-kahs, ess-tee bee-ba-loy!)

2. *Perform the Banishing Ritual of the Pentagram. Use either dagger or index finger. (See Appendix Five.)*

3. *Perform the Banishing Ritual of the Hexagram. Use the unicursal Hexagram only; the other forms are superfluous. (See Appendix Five.)*

4. *Go to South of Altar. Pick up stick of incense, the book of matches, or the Fire Wand. Wave it three times in front of Tablet or Sigil, hold above head, and move slowly around the perimeter of room, deosil (clockwise), vibrating or humming:*

5. 'And when, after all the phantoms have vanished, thou shalt see that holy and formless fire, that fire which darts and flashes through the hidden depths of the Universe, hear thou the Voice of Fire.'

6. *On reaching South, shake fire symbol three times before the Tablet or Sigil, then make a large circle, tracing invoking Pentagram of Fire within it, then sign of Leo as Fire Kerub in centre, saying:*

7. 'OIP TEAA PEDOCE (oh-ee-pay tay-ah-ah pay-doh-kay). In the names and letters of the Great Southern Quadrangle, I invoke ye, ye Angels of the Watchtower of the South.'

8. *Replace fire symbol. Go to West, pick up glass of Water, sprinkle a few drops in front of Tablet or Sigil, and circumambulate clockwise, saying:*

9. 'So therefore first, the priest who governeth the works of fire must sprinkle with the lustral water of the loud resounding sea.'

10. *On returning to West, sprinkle Water three times before Tablet or Sigil, and with cup make circle, with the Invoking Water Pentagram within it, then Eagle Kerub in Centre, vibrating:*

11. 'EMPEH ARSEL GAIOL (em-pay-hay ar-sel gah-ee-ohl). In the names and letters of the Great Western Quadrangle, I invoke ye, ye Angels of the Watchtower of the West.'

12. *Replace Cup. Walk clockwise to East of Altar, take Fan or Air dagger, shake three times before Tablet, then circumambulate, saying:*

13. 'Such a fire existeth, extending through the rushing of Air. Or even a fire formless, whence cometh the image of a voice. Or even a flashing light, abounding, revolving, whirling forth, crying aloud.'

14. *On returning to East, strike Air in front of Tablet three times with fan or dagger; then make circle, with Invoking Air Pentagram within it, with sign of Aquarius for Air Kerub in centre, saying:*

15. 'ORO IBAH AOZPI (eh-roh ee-bah-hay ah-oh-zohd-pee). In the names and letters of the Great Eastern Quadrangle, I invoke ye, ye Angels of the Watchtower of the East.'

16. *Replace Air symbol. Walk clockwise to North. Pick up Earth Pentacle or saucer of bread and salt. Sprinkle salt or shake instrument in front of Tablet three times. Then circumambulate, saying:*

17. 'Stoop not down into that darkly splendid world wherein continually lieth a faithless depth and Hades wrapped in gloom, delighting in unintelligible images, precipitous, winding; a black ever-rolling abyss, ever espousing a body unluminous, formless and void.'

18. *On returning to North, shake instrument in front of Tablet; then make Circle with Invoking Earth Pentagram within it, with Sign of Taurus for Earth Kerub in centre, saying:*

19. 'EMOR DIAL HECTEGA (ee-mor dee-ahl hec-tay-gah). In the names and letters of the Great Northern Quadrangle, I invoke ye, ye Angels of the Watchtower of the North.'

20. *Replace instrument. Walk around Altar to West and then face East. Pick up flower, or use index finger to describe Invoking Pentagrams of Spirit (within circle), both active and passive, saying:*

21. 'EXARP (Ex-ar-pay). BITOM (bay-ee-toh-em). NANTA (en-ah-en-tah). HCOMA (hay-coh-mah). In the names and letters

of the mystical Tablet of Union, I invoke ye, ye divine forces of the Spirit of Life.'

22. *Replace flower. Make the Portal Sign of the Rending of the Veil. Stretch hands before you, then separate them sharply as if opening a curtain. Then say:*

23. 'I invoke ye, ye Angels of the celestial spheres, whose dwelling is in the invisible. Ye are the guardians of the gates of the Universe, be ye also the guardians of this mystic sphere. Keep far removed the evil and the unbalanced. Strengthen and inspire me so that I may preserve unsullied this abode of the mysteries of the eternal Gods. Let my sphere be pure and holy so that I may enter in and become a partaker of the secrets of the Light Divine.'

24. *Go to North-east, and say:*

'The visible Sun is the dispenser of Light to the Earth. Let me therefore form a vortex in this chamber that the Invisible Sun of the Spirit may shine therein from above.'

25. *Circumambulate three times clockwise beginning at the East. Make the Projecting Sign (throw arms forward straight from the shoulders, head bowed between them) each time you pass the East. Return to the West of the Altar and utter the Adoration. Make the Projecting Sign at the end of the first three lines. Make the Sign of Silence at the end of the fourth line — right arm hanging by your side, raise index and third fingers of left hand to the lips.*

> 'Holy art thou, Lord of the Universe.
> Holy art thou, whom Nature hath not formed.
> Holy art thou, the Vast and the Mighty One.
> Lord of the Light and the Darkness.'

At this point state in your own words the purpose for which you are performing this ceremony.

26. *Sit quietly facing the East, not passively, but in stillness, attempting to feel the presence of the spirit above you, around you and within you.*

27. *When you feel ready, after whatever spiritual exercise you feel impelled to do, close the Temple by reversing the circumambulations (widdershins), making the Projecting Sign each time you pass the East. Then perform the Banishing Rituals of the Pentagram and the Hexagram.*

28. *Conclude with the following:*

'I now release any spirits that may have been imprisoned by this ceremony. Depart in peace to your abodes and habitations, and go with the blessing of YEHESHUAH YEHOVASHAH (yuh-hesh-you-ah yuh-hoh-vah-shah).'

Pause.

'I now declare this Temple duly closed.'

CHAPTER III

Opening by Watchtower: First Elaboration

In giving the rubric of the Watchtower Ritual, each individual segment is numbered. My purpose in doing this was to make it easy for the student to insert, in the right place, any new addition or invocation that he chooses to employ.

The opening announcement is to proclaim that the room is duly consecrated. It is holy ground, and that in effect, the profane or those not connected with the work about to be commenced, should depart. In *Liber Israfel*, Crowley omitted this phrase and employed in its stead: 'Procul, o Procul este profani!'

The Banishing Ritual of the Pentagram is fully explained in Vol. III of *The Golden Dawn*. This should be consulted and read before proceeding further. Also see p. 107 of Vol. I of the same series. An earlier book of mine, *The Middle Pillar* goes into considerable detail as to how this ritual should be done. Detailed instructions will be found in the Appendix.

So far as the Banishing Ritual of the Hexagram is concerned, again I have to refer the student to Vol. III of *The Golden Dawn*. The instruction describes four forms of the hexagram to be used. After many years of use, I confess to finding little value in such detail. The only hexagram of value is that described on p. 29 of Vol. III, the so-called second form, supposedly having an affinity with the South. I suggest therefore that only this hexagram be used, if you use it at all.

As an aside, it should be mentioned that to invoke the Sun by the method described, requires the use in each quarter of all six hexagrams attributed to the other planets. This makes the whole process far too long, tedious and laborious. Crowley has developed what he calls a unicursal hexagram, one that is described with a single line, with no break. It is possible to develop a form of this particular hexagram for the invocation or banishing of the Sun, etc., instead of the more tedious Golden Dawn method. But of this, see the Appendix where this is worked out experimentally and in full.

The instruction also directs that the Signs of the 5=6 grade be used before and after the invoking or banishing ritual. These are sometimes called the LVX signs. While it is true that they are reproduced in one of the appendices, nevertheless, if the student finds them too terribly complicated to use at the outset, omit them altogether. Instead, the opening of the Pentagram ritual may be used – that is, the Qabalistic Cross. It is simple and meaningful and uncomplicated. (See Appendix Five for full instructions.)

With (4) begins the Watchtower Ritual proper. When the student, by practice, has become expert in its use, he may start the process of enlarging the scope of the ritual. He could insert the following method of invocation, omitting entirely section (7).

> (7) 'Let us adore the Lord and King of Fire. YOD HEH VAU HEH TZABAOTH. Blessed be Thou – Leader of Armies is Thy Name. Amen!'

Here the Fire Sign is given. Hands joined in front of the forehead, so that the two thumbs touching, form the base of a triangle, completed by the fingers pointing upwards and touching. The student makes the Invoking Pentagrams of Fire and Spirit Active in a circle before the Fire Tablet.

> 'And the Elohim said: "Let us make Adam in our own image, after our own likeness and let him have dominion. In the name of ELOHIM, mighty and ruling, and in the name YOD HEH VAU HEH TZABAOTH, Spirits of Fire, adore your Creator".'

Student makes the sign of Leo before the Tablet with the wand or match.

> 'And in the name of MICHAEL, the Great Archangel of Fire, and in the Kerubic Sign of Leo, the Lion, Spirits of Fire, adore your Creator.'

Here the student makes the sign of a cross with the same instrument.

'In the names and letters of the Great Southern Quadrangle Spirits of Fire, adore your Creator!'

Hold the instrument on high and wave it before Tablet.

'In the Three Great Secret Names of God borne upon the Banners of the South – OIP TEAA PEDOCE, Spirits of Fire, adore your Creator!

And in the name of EDELPERNA, Great King of the South, Spirits of Fire, adore your Creator!'

This is the basic pattern that will be followed with each of the elements and each cardinal quarter. Each will be taken from the appropriate elemental initiatory grade. Each presents the classical and ideal form of invocation. Notice, too, that the Watchtower Ritual invokes the angels of the Watchtowers or Tablets in the order of TETRAGRAMMATON, that is, Fire (South) = YOD, Water (West) = HEH, Air (East) = VAU and Earth (North) = HEH Final.

So for (11), which we omit, there will be substituted the following from the 3=8 or Practicus Ritual.

'Let us adore the Lord and King of Water. ELOHIM TZABAOTH – ELOHIM of Hosts! Glory be unto the RUACH ELOHIM who moved upon the face of the waters of Creation. Amen!'

Salute with the Water Sign, hands are placed over chest, thumbs joined to form a straight line, fingers pointing downwards to form the descending water triangle. Take the Cup of Water, and trace the Invoking Circle and Pentagrams of Water and Spirit Passive in front of the Tablet or Sigil.

And the ELOHIM said: 'Let us make Adam in our image, after our likeness, and let him have dominion over the fish of the sea. In the name of AL strong and Powerful, and in the name of ELOHIM TZABAOTH, Spirits of Water adore your Creator!'

With the same Cup, the student traces before the Tablet, the Sign of the Eagle, the Kerub of Scorpio.

'In the name of GABRIEL, the Great Archangel of Water, and in the Sign of the Eagle, Spirits of Water, adore your Creator!'

Make a Cross with the Cup.

'In the names and letters of the Great Western Quadrangle, Spirits of Water adore your Creator!'

Hold Cup on high and sprinkle water in three directions before Tablet.

'In the Three Great Secret Names of God borne upon the banners of the West, EMPEH ARSEL GAIOL, Spirits of Water adore your Creator! In the name of RA-AGIOSEL, Great King of the West, Spirits of Water adore your Creator!'

For (15) the same procedure is followed. It is omitted and replaced by the following, extrapolated from the 2=9 Ritual of Theoricus.

'Let us adore the Lord and King of Air!'

Student makes a circle with Fan or Air Dagger in front of Air Tablet in East.

'SHADDAI EL CHAI, Almighty and Everlasting – everliving be Thy name, ever magnified in the life of all. Amen!'

Student salutes with Air sign in front of Tablet. Tilt the head slightly backwards, and raise arms up like Atlas holding up the world in his hands. Then make Invoking Pentagrams of Air and Spirit Active within a circle before the Air Tablet.

And the ELOHIM said: 'Let us make Adam in our image, after our likeness, and let him have dominion over the fowl of the Air.'

'In the name YOD HEH VAU HEH and in the name SHADDAI EL CHAI, Spirits of Air, adore your Creator!'

Make the Kerubic Sign of Air, Aquarius, in front of Tablet with the instrument.

'In the name of RAPHAEL, the Great Archangel of Air, and in the Kerubic Sign of the Head of the Man, Spirits of Air adore your Creator!'

Make Cross with the instrument.

'In the names and letters of the Great Eastern Quadrangle, Spirits of Air adore your Creator!'

Hold fan on high and shake it three times before Tablet.

'In the Three Great Secret Holy Names of God borne upon the banners of the East, ORO IBAH AOZPI, Spirits of Air, adore your Creator! In the Name of BATAIVAH, Great King of the East, Spirits of Air, adore your Creator!'

For (19) the same procedure is followed. It is wholly deleted and replaced by the fuller invocation extrapolated from the 1=10 or Zelator Ritual.

'Let us adore the Lord and King of Earth. ADONAI HA-ARETZ, ADONAI MELEKH. Unto Thee be the Kingdom and the Power and the Glory.'

At this point the student should make the Qabalistic Cross.

He then makes Cross and Circle with instrument, before the Earth Tablet.

'The Rose of Sharon and the Lily of the Valley, Amen.'
'Let the Earth adore ADONAI.'

The Invoking Pentagrams of Earth and Spirit Passive within a circle should be traced at this point.

And the ELOHIM said: 'Let us make Adam in our image, after our likeness and let him have dominion over the fish of the sea and over the fowl of the air and over the cattle and over all the earth, and over every creeping thing that creepeth over the earth. And the ELOHIM created ETH HA-ADAM in their own image, in the image of the ELOHIM created they him. In the name of ADONAI MELEKH and of the Bride and Queen of the Kingdom, Spirits of Earth adore ADONAI!'

Tracing the Kerubic sign of Earth, Taurus, within the Pentagram, say:

'In the name of AURIEL, the Great Archangel of Earth and by the Sign of the Head of the OX, Spirits of Earth, adore ADONAI!'

Sprinkling some of the salt towards the Tablet, he says:

'In the Names and Letters of the Great Northern Quadrangle, Spirits of Earth, adore ADONAI! In the Three Great Secret Holy Names of God borne upon the Banners of the North, EMOR DIAL HECTEGA, and in the name of IC ZOD HEH CHAL, Great King of the North, Spirits of Earth adore your Creator!'

Make the saluting sign of Earth.

For the invocation of the fifth element, the procedure varies slightly from what has gone on before. The action in (22) remains, but immediately following, the Enochian Invocation from the Portal Grade is vibrated:

OL SONUF VAORSAGI GOHO IADA BALTA. ELEXARPEH COMANANU TABITOM. ZODAKARA, EKA ZODAKARE OD ZODAMERANU. ODO KIKLE QAA PIAP PIAMOEL OD VAOAN.

The translation of this invocation is more or less as follows: 'I reign over you, saith the God of Justice. ELEXARPEH COMANANU TABITOM. (These are the three Angels who rule over the Tablet of Union.) Move therefore and show yourselves. Appear unto us; open the mysteries of your Creation, the balance of Righteousness and Truth.'

The proper pronunciation of the Enochian has already been given in Chapter II.

This completes the first set of additions and modifications of the Ritual. Since practice makes perfect, use it extensively and frequently until technical perfection is attained. Then, when no further conscious attention need be given to technique, it may be that the student will become more conscious of what the ritual strives to accomplish.

CHAPTER IV

Opening by Watchtower: Second Elaboration

The process of expansion of the basic ritual form continues with the addition of the elemental prayers. In each of the four elemental grades of the Order, the ceremony closes by the exhortation of the Hierophant that the Lord and King of the Element be adored. I have long felt that these are amongst the most beautiful and moving prayers or adorations within the structure of the Order Rituals. It was this that originally moved me many years ago to use them with the Watchtower Ritual, either in their complete form or abbreviated to a few lines or sentences.

I give them as follows in the order in which they are used in the Ritual. After point (7), which completes the invocation of the element of Fire, the following prayer is appropriate:

> '*Immortal, eternal, ineffable and uncreated Father of all, borne upon the chariot of worlds which ever roll in ceaseless motion.* Ruler over the ethereal vastness where the throne of thy power is raised, from the Summit of which thine eyes behold all and thy pure and holy ears hear all, *help us, thy children, whom thou hast loved since the birth of the ages of time! Thy majesty, golden, vast and eternal, shineth above the heaven of stars. Above them art thou exalted.*
>
> 'O thou flashing fire, there thou illuminest all things with thine insupportable glory, whence flow the ceaseless streams of splendour which nourish thine infinite spirit. This infinite spirit nourisheth all and maketh that inexhaustible treasure of generation which ever encompasseth thee, replete with the numberless forms wherewith thou has filled it from the beginning.
>
> 'From this spirit arise those most holy kings who are around thy throne and who compose thy court. O Universal Father, one and alone! Father alike of immortals and mortals. Thou has specially created

powers similar unto thy thought eternal and unto they venerable essence. Thou has established them above the Angels who announce thy will to the world!

'Lastly, thou hast created us as a third order in our elemental empire. There *our continual exercise is to praise and to adore thy desires; there we ceaselessly burn with eternal aspirations unto thee, O Father! O Mother of Mothers! O archetype eternal of maternity and love! O Son, the flower of all sons! Form of all forms! Soul, spirit, harmony and numeral of all things, Amen!*'

Some parts of the above prayer are italicized. This is merely to suggest an abbreviated form of the prayer. However, the student may disregard this suggestion and construct his own abbreviation, should he desire one.

Immediately after point (11) is the proper place for the Prayer of the Water Elementals or Undines.

'Terrible King of the sea, thou who holdest the keys of the cataracts of heaven, and who enclosest the subterranean waters in the cavernous hollows of earth. *King of the deluge and of the rains of spring.* Thou who openest the sources of the rivers and of the fountains. *Thou who commandest moisture which is, as it were, the Blood of the Earth, to become the Sap of the Plants, we adore thee and we invoke thee. Speak Thou unto us, thy mobile and changeful creatures in the great tempests and we shall tremble before thee. Speak to us also in the murmur of the limpid waters, and we shall desire thy love.*

'O vastness wherein all the rivers of being seek to lose themselves – which renew themselves ever in thee! O thou Ocean of infinite perfection! O height which reflectest thyself in the depth! O depth which exhalest into the height! *Lead us into immortality through sacrifice, that we may be found worthy to offer one day unto thee, the water, the blood and the tears, for the remission of sins, Amen!*'

Point (15) is the place for the insertion of the Prayer of the Sylphs, or the elementals of Air:

'*Spirit of Life. Spirit of wisdom, whose breath giveth forth and withdraweth the form of all things.* Thou, before whom the life of beings is but a shadow which changeth, and a vapour which passeth. Thou who mountest upon the clouds and who walkest upon the wings of the wind. Thou who breathest forth thy breath, and endless space is peopled. Thou, who drawest in thy breath, and all that cometh from thee, returneth unto thee!

'Ceaseless motion, in eternal stability, be thou eternally blessed! *We praise thee and we bless thee in the changeless empire of created light, of shades, of reflections and of images.* And we aspire without cessation unto thy immutable and imperishable brilliance.

'Let the ray of thy intelligence and the warmth of thy love penetrate even unto *us!* Then that which is volatile shall be fixed; the shadow shall be a body; the spirit of air shall be a soul; the dream shall be a thought. *And no more shall we be swept away by the tempest, but we shall hold the bridles of the winged steeds of dawn. And we shall direct the course of the evening breeze to fly before thee!*

'O spirit of spirits! O eternal soul of souls! O imperishable breath of life! O creative sigh! O mouth which breathest forth and withdrawest the life of all beings, in the flux and reflux of thine eternal word, which is the divine ocean of movement and of truth!'

Point (19) is the place to insert the Prayer of the Gnomes or Earth elementals.

'O *invisible king, who, taking the Earth for foundation, didst hollow its depths to fill them with thy almighty power.* Thou whose name shaketh the arches of the world. Thou who causest the seven metals to flow in the veins of the rocks, king of the seven lights, *rewarder of the subterranean workers, lead us into the desirable air and into the realm of splendour.*

'*We watch and we labour unceasingly. We seek and we hope, by the twelve stones of the Holy City, by the buried talismans, by the axis of the loadstone which passes through the centre of the Earth!* O Lord, O Lord, O Lord! Have pity upon those who suffer. Expand our hearts, unbind and upraise our minds, enlarge our natures.

'O Stability and motion! O darkness veiled in brilliance! O day clothed in night! O master who never dost withhold the wages of thy workman! O silver whiteness. O golden splendour! O crown of living harmonious diamond! *Thou who wearest the heavens on thy finger like a ring of sapphire! Thou who hidest beneath the earth in the kingdom of gems, the marvellous seed of the stars! Live, reign and be Thou the eternal dispenser of the treasures whereof Thou hast made us the wardens.*'

After point (24) there can be inserted some of the lovely speeches from the 5=6 Ritual which transforms this ritual from merely a means of opening the temple to one of spiritual aspiration and development. For example:

'I am the Resurrection and the Life. He that believeth on me, though he were dead, yet shall he live, and whosoever liveth and believeth on me shall never die.

'I am the First and I am the Last. I am He that liveth and was dead, and behold! I am alive for evermore and hold the keys of Hell and of Death. For I know that my Redeemer liveth and he shall stand at the latter day upon the earth. I am the Way, the Truth and the Life. No man cometh unto the Father but by me.

'I am the purified. I have passed through the gates of darkness unto Light. I have fought upon Earth for good. I have finished my work. I have entered into the invisible.

'I am the Sun in his rising, passed through the hour of cloud and of night. I am Amoun, the concealed one, the Opener of the Day. I am Osiris Onnophris, the Justified One, Lord of Life, triumphant over death. There is no part of me which is not of the Gods.

'I am the Preparer of the Pathway, the Rescuer unto the Light. I am the Reconciler with the Ineffable, the Dweller of the Invisible. Let the White Light of the Divine Spirit descend.'

There is a final peroration from the Bornless Ritual which is a paean of triumph and attainment to be used as the climax of the entire Ritual.

'I am He, the Bornless Spirit, having Sight in the Feet, Strong, and the Immortal Fire.

'I am He, the Truth.

'I am He, who hate that evil should be wrought in the world.

'I am He that lighteneth and thundereth.

'I am He from whom is the shower of the Life of Earth.

'I am He, the Begetter and Manifester unto the Light.

'I am He, the Grace of the World.

'The Heart Girt with a Serpent is my Name.

'Come thou forth and follow me, and make all spirits subject unto me so that every spirit of the firmament and of the ether, upon the earth and under the earth, on dry land and in the water, of whirling air and of rushing fire, and every spell and scourge of God, the Vast One, may be made obedient unto me. IAO. SABAO. Such are the words.'

After contemplating the glory for some while, go to the West of the Altar, facing East, and give thanks either in your own words or with the following prayer:

'Unto Thee, sole wise, sole eternal and sole merciful One, be the praise and the glory for ever. Who has permitted me, who now standeth humbly before Thee, to enter thus far into the sanctuary of they mysteries. Not unto me, but unto Thy name be the glory.

'Let the influence of thy divine ones descend upon my head, and teach me the value of self-sacrifice, so that I shrink not in the hour of trial, but that thus my name may be written on high, and my Genius may stand in the presence of the Holy Ones – in that hour when the Son of Man is invoked before the Lord of Spirits and His name in the presence of the Ancient of Days.'

The following chapter will consolidate all the different elements so far assembled. They will be integrated, as you will see, into a perfectly workable and inspiring ritual which the good student could well decide to use on and off for the rest of his life.

CHAPTER V

Completed Ritual

1. *Stand at Altar, facing East and announce:*

   HEKAS, HEKAS, ESTE BEBELOI!

2. *Perform the Banishing Ritual of the Pentagram.*
3. *Perform the Banishing Ritual of the Hexagram.*
4. *Go to South of Altar, pick up symbol of Fire, hold it above head and circumambulate the room clockwise, vibrating:*
5. 'And when after all the phantoms have vanished, thou shalt see that holy and formless fire, that fire which darts and flashes through the hidden depths of the universe, hear thou the voice of Fire.'
6. *On reaching the South, face the Tablet or Sigil and say:*

   'Let us adore the Lord and King of Fire. YOD HE VAU HEH TZABAOTH (Yod-hay-vahv-hay Tzah-bah-oth). Blessed be Thou – Leader of Armies is Thy name. Amen!'

   Here the Fire sign is given. Hands joined in front of the forehead so that the two thumbs touching form the base of a triangle, completed by the fingers pointing upward and touching. Take the Fire symbol from Altar and make large Circle and Invoking Pentagrams of Active Spirit and Fire before the Sigil.

   'And ELOHIM (ay-loh-heem) said Let us make Adam in our own image, after our own likeness, and let him have dominion. In the name of ELOHIM, mighty and ruling, and in the name YOD HEH VAU HEH TZABAOTH, Spirits of Fire adore your Creator.'

Student makes the sign Leo before the Tablet with the Wand or other fire symbol.

'And in the name of MICHAEL (Mee-chah-ale), the Great Archangel of Fire, and in the Kerubic Sign of Leo the Lion, Spirits of Fire, adore your Creator.'

Here the student makes the sign of the Cross with the same instrument.

'In the names and letters of the Great Southern Quadrangle Spirits of Fire, adoré your Creator!'

Hold the instrument on high, waving it thrice before Tablet or Sigil.

'In the Three Great Secret Holy Names of God borne upon the Banners of the South – OIP TEAA PEDOCE (Oh-ee-pay tay-ah-ah pay-doh-kay), and in the name of EDELPERNA (ay-dell-per-nah), Great King of the South, I now invoke the Angels of the Watchtower of the South.'

Adopt once more the Fire Sign, and say:

'Immortal, eternal, ineffable and uncreated Father of all, borne upon the chariot of worlds, which ever roll in ceaseless motion, help us thy children, whom Thou hast loved since the birth of the ages of time! Thy majesty, golden, vast and eternal, shineth above the heaven of stars. Above them art Thou exalted. Our continual exercise is to praise and to adore Thy desires; there we ceaselessly burn with eternal aspirations unto Thee. O Father! O Mother of mothers! O Son, the flower of all sons! Form of all forms! Soul, spirit, harmony and numeral of all things. Amen!'

8. *Replace the Fire symbol on altar. Go to West, pick up glass of water, circumambulate clockwise, saying:*

9. 'So therefore first the priest who governeth the works of Fire must sprinkle with the lustral water of the loud resounding sea.'

10. *On reaching the West, sprinkle water thrice facing the quarter, and vibrate:*

'Let us adore the Lord and King of Water. ELOHIM

TZABAOTH (ay-loh-heem tza-bay-oth), ELOHIM of Hosts!
Glory be unto the RUACH ELOHIM (roo-ahk ayloh-heem)
who moved upon the face of the waters of Creation. Amen!'

*Salute with the Water Sign. Hands are placed over chest, thumbs joined
to form a straight line, fingers pointing downwards to form the descending
water triangle. Take the Cup of Water and trace the Circle and Invoking
Pentagrams of Spirit Passive and of Water in front of the Sigil.*

'And ELOHIM said: "Let us make Adam in our image, after
our likeness, and let him have dominion over the fish of the sea.
In the name of AL (ale) strong and powerful, and in the name
of ELOHIM TZABAOTH, Spirits of Water adore your
Creator!" '

*With the same Cup, the student traces the Sign of the Eagle, the Kerub
of Scorpio.*

'In the name of GABRIEL (gah-bree-ale) the Great Archangel
of Water, and in the Sign of the Eagle, Spirits of Water, adore
your Creator!'

Make Cross with the Cup.

'In the names and letters of the Great Northern Quadrangle,
Spirits of Water, adore your Creator!'

*Hold Cup on high and sprinkle water in three directions before Tablet or
Sigil.*

'In the Three Great Secret Holy Names of God borne upon the
banners of the West, EMPEH ARSEL GAIOL (em-pay-hay
ar-sell gah-ee-ohl) and in the name of RA-AGIOSEL (rah-ah-
gee-oh-sel), Great King of the West, I invoke ye, ye Angels of
the Watchtower of the West!'

Assume Water Sign and say:

'Terrible King of the Sea, King of the deluge and of the rains of
spring. Thou who commandest moisture which is, as it were,
the blood of the Earth, to become the Sap of the Plants, we
adore Thee and we invoke Thee. Speak Thou unto us, thy

mobile and changeful creatures in the great tempests and we shall tremble before Thee. Speak to us also in the murmur of the limpid waters, and we shall desire Thy love. Lead us unto immortality through sacrifice, that we may be found worthy to offer one day unto Thee, the water, the blood and the tears for the remission of sins. Amen!'

12. *Replace the Cup. Walk clockwise to the East of the Altar, and take up the Fan or Air symbol, shake thrice in front of the Tablet, circumambulating, saying:*

13. 'Such a Fire existeth, extending through the rushing of air, or even a fire formless whence cometh the image of a voice, or even a flashing light, abounding, revolving, whirling forth, crying aloud.'

14. *On reaching East, strike Air weapon in front of the Tablet or Sigil three times, saying:*

15. 'Let us adore the Lord and King of Air. SHADDAI EL CHAI (shah-dye ale khye), Almighty and Everlasting – ever living be Thy Name, ever magnified in the life of all. Amen!'

Student salutes with Air Sign. Raise hands to level of ears, palms up as in classical picture of Atlas holding world up with his hands. Then with Air instrument make Circle with Invoking Pentagrams of Spirit Active and of Air before the Tablet or Sigil.

'And the ELOHIM said: "Let us make Adam in our image, after our likeness, and let him have dominion over the fowl of the air. In the name of YOD HEH VAU HEH and in the name of SHADDAI EL CHAI, Spirits of Air, adore your Creator!" '

Make the Kerubic Sign of Air, Aquarius, in front of Tablet with Air symbol.

'In the name of RAPHAEL (rah-phah-ale) the Great Archangel of Air, and in the Kerubic sign of the Head of the Man, Spirits of Air, adore your Creator!'

Make Cross with the instrument.

'In the names and letters of the Great Eastern Quadrangle, Spirits of Air adore your Creator!'

Hold symbol on high, shaking it thrice before Tablet.

'In the Three Great Secret Holy Names of God borne upon the banners of the East, ORO IBAH AOZPI (oh-roh ee-bah-hay ah-oh-zohd-pee) and in the name of BATAIVAH (bah-tah-ee-vah-hay) I invoke ye, ye angels of the Watchtower of the East.'

Assume Air sign, and say:

'Spirit of Life, Spirit of Wisdom, whose breath giveth forth and withdraweth the form of all things. We praise Thee and we bless Thee in the changeless empire of created light, of shades, of reflections and of images. And we aspire without cessation unto thy immutable and imperishable brilliance.

Let the ray of Thy intelligence and warmth of Thy love penetrate even unto us. And no more shall we be swept away by the tempest, but we shall hold the bridles of the winged steeds of dawn. And we shall direct the course of the evening breeze to fly before Thee; the divine ocean of movement and of truth.

16. *Replace symbol on Altar. Walk clockwise to North, and pick up Earth symbol, shaking it thrice in front of the Tablet, and circumambulate, saying:*

17. 'Stoop not down into that darkly splendid world wherein continually lieth a faithless depth and Hades wrapped in gloom, delighting in unintelligible images, precipitous, winding, a black, ever-rolling abyss, ever espousing a body unluminous, formless and void.'

18. *On reaching North, again shake instrument or sprinkle salt thrice in front of Tablet, saying:*

'Let us adore the Lord and King of Earth. ADONAI HA-ARETZ, ADONAI MELEKH (ah-doh-nye hah-ahr-retz, ah-doh-nye may-lekh). Unto Thee be the Kingdom and the Power and the Glory.'

Student salutes with Earth sign. Raise right arm stiffly at 45° angle. With Earth symbol make Circle and Invoking Pentagrams of Spirit Passive and of Earth, before the Tablet.

'And the ELOHIM said: "Let us make Adam in our image, after our likeness and let him have dominion over the fish of the sea, and over the fowl of the air, and over the cattle and over all the earth, and over every creeping thing that creepeth over the earth." And the ELOHIM created ETH HA-ADAM in their own image, in the image of the ELOHIM created they him. In the name of ADONAI MELEKH and of the Bride and Queen of the Kingdom, Spirits of Earth adore ADONAI!'

Tracing the Kerubic Sign of Earth, Taurus, within the Pentagram, say:

'In the name of AURIEL (awe-ree-ale), the Great Archangel of Earth, and by the Sign of the Head of the Ox, Spirits of Earth adore ADONAI!'

Here student makes Cross and Circle with instrument before Earth Tablet.

'The Rose of Sharon and the Lily of the Valley, Amen! Let the Earth adore ADONAI!'

Sprinkling some of the salt towards the Tablet thrice, say:

'In the Names and letters of the Great Northern Quadrangle, Spirits of Earth, adore ADONAI! In the Three Great Secret Holy Names of God borne upon the banners of the North, EMOR DIAL HECTEGA (ee-mor dee-ahl heck-tay-gah) and in the name of IC ZOD HEH CHAL (ick-zohd-hay-khal), Great King of the North, I invoke ye, ye angels of the Watch-towers of the North.'

Make the Earth Sign, saying:

'O Invisible King who, taking the Earth for foundation, didst hollow its depths to fill them with Thy almighty power. Thou whose Name shaketh the arches of the world, rewarder of the subterranean workers, lead us into the desirable air and into the realm of splendour. We watch and we labour unceasingly. We seek and we hope, by the twelve stones of the Holy City, by the buried talismans, by the axis of the lodestone which passes through the centre of the Earth! O Lord! O Lord! O Lord! Have pity upon those who suffer. Expand our hearts, unbind and upraise our minds, enlarge our natures. Thou who wearest the heavens on thy finger like a ring of sapphire! Thou who hidest beneath the earth in the kingdom of gems, the marvellous seed of the stars! Live, reign, and be Thou the Eternal Dispenser of the Treasures whereof Thou hast made us the wardens.'

Replace Earth symbol. Walk around Altar to the West so you face East. Pick up flower, or use index finger to describe both Invoking Pentagrams of Spirit, Active and Passive, saying:

21. 'EXARP (Ex-ar-pay). BITOM (bay-ee-toh-em). NANTA (en-ah-en-tah). HCOMA (heh-coh-mah). In the names and letters of the mystical Tablet of Union, I invoke ye, ye divine forces of the Spirit of Life.'

22. *Replace flower. Make the Portal Sign of the Rending of the Veil; stretch hands before you and separate them sharply as if opening a curtain. Then say:*

'OL SONUF VAORSAGI GOHO IADA BALTA (oh-ell soh-noof vay-oh-air-sah-jee goh-hoh ee-ahdah bal-tah). ELEXARPEH COMANANU TABITOM (el-ex-ar-pay-hay co-mah-nah-noo tah-bee-toh-em). ZODAKARA EKA ZODAKARE OD ZODAMERANU (zohd-ah-kah-rah eh-kah zoh-ah-kah-ray oh-dah zohd-ah-mer-ah-noo). ODO KIKLE QAA PIAPE PIAMOEL OD VAOAN (oh-doh kee-klay kah-ah pee-ah-pay pee-ah-moh-ell oh-dah vay-oh-ah-noo).'

23. 'I invoke ye, ye Angels of the celestial spheres whose dwelling is in the Invisible. Ye are the guardians of the gates of the Universe, be ye also the guardians of this mystic sphere. Keep far removed the evil and the unbalanced. Strengthen and inspire me so that I may preserve unsullied this abode of the mysteries of the Eternal Gods. Let my sphere be pure and holy so that I may enter in and become a partaker of the secrets of the Light divine.'

24. *Now say:*

'The visible Sun is the dispenser of Light to the Earth. Let me therefore form a vortex in this chamber that the Invisible Sun of the Spirit may shine thereinto from above.'

25. *Circumambulate three times clockwise, beginning at the East. Make the Projecting Sign each time you pass the East. Return to the Altar and utter the Adoration. Make the projecting Sign at the end of each of the first three lines. Make the Sign of Silence at the end of the fourth line.*

'Holy art thou, Lord of the Universe.
Holy art thou, whom Nature hath not formed.
Holy art thou, the Vast and the Mighty One.
Lord of the Light and the Darkness.'

At this point state in your own words the purpose for which you are performing this ceremony.

Still facing East, say:

'I am the Resurrection and the Life. He that believeth in me, though he were dead, yet shall he live, and whosoever liveth and believeth on me shall never die. I am the First and I am the Last. I am He that liveth and was dead, and behold! I am alive forevermore and hold the keys of hell and of death. For I know that my Redeemer liveth and he shall stand at the latter day upon the earth. I am the Way, the Truth and the Life. No man cometh unto the Father but by me. I am the purified. I have passed through the gates of darkness unto Light. I have fought upon earth for good. I have finished my work. I have entered into the invisible.

I am the Sun in his rising, passed through the hour of cloud and of night. I am AMOUN the concealed one, the Opener of the Day. I am OSIRIS ONNOPHRIS the Justified One, Lord of Life, triumphant over death. There is no part of me which is not of the Gods.

I am the Preparer of the Pathway, the Rescuer unto the Light. I am the Reconciler with the Ineffable, the Dweller of the Invisible. Let the White Light of the Divine Spirit descend.

26. *Sit quietly facing the East, not passively, but in stillness, meditating and attempting to feel the presence above you, around you and within you.*

27. *When you feel ready, after whatever spiritual exercise you may feel impelled to do and after whatever spiritual realization you may have followed, use the final peroration from the Bornless Ritual, a paean of triumph and attainment, which may be used as the climax of the entire Ritual.*

28. 'I am He, the Bornless Spirit, having sight in the feet, strong and the Immortal Fire.

I am He, the Truth.

I am He, who hate that evil should be wrought in the world.

I am He that lighteneth and thundereth.

I am He from whom is the shower of the Life of Earth.

I am He, the Begetter and Manifester unto the Light.

I am He, the Grace of the World.

The Heart girt with a Serpent is my Name.

Come thou forth and follow me and make all spirits subject unto me, so that every spirit of the firmament and of the ether, upon the earth and under the earth, on dry land and in the water, of whirling air and of rushing fire, and every spell and scourge of God, the Vast one, may be made obedient unto me, IAO SABAO (ee-ah-oh sah-bah-oh). Such are the words.'

29. *After contemplating the glory for some while, go to the West of the Altar, facing East and give thanks.*

30. 'Unto Thee, sole wise, sole eternal and sole merciful One, be the praise and glory for ever, Who has permitted me who now standeth humbly before Thee, to enter thus far into the sanctuary of Thy mysteries. Not unto me, but unto Thy name be the glory. Let the influence of thy divine ones descend upon my head, and teach me the value of self-sacrifice so that I shrink not in the hour of trial, but that thus my name may be written on high and my Genius stand in the presence of the Holy Ones. In that hour when the Son of Man is invoked before the Lord of Spirits and His name in the presence of the Ancient of Days.'

31. *Close the Temple by reversing the circumambulation and by the Banishing Rituals of the Pentagram and the Hexagram. Then conclude with the following.*

32. 'I now release any spirits that may have been imprisoned by this ceremony. Depart in peace to your abodes and habitations and go with the blessing of YEHESHUAH YEHOVASHAH forever.

I now declare this Temple duly closed.'

CHAPTER VI

A Magical Eucharist

This ceremony is a sequel to that already described and outlined in Chapter II, points 1 to 26 inclusive. It describes in detail a simple form of Eucharist which can be used either by one person alone, or in concert with a group.

Much of the magical theory of the Eucharist has already been worked out in *Magic in East and West* to be found in my book *Foundations of Practical Magic* (Aquarian Press, 1979). Repetition is therefore unnecessary. But the student should certainly re-read that essay before attempting this ritual. Some understanding of the theory is a prerequisite if it is to make any sense.

The altar top is arranged as follows:

East

Dagger and Flower

North		*South*
Pantacle	Cross	Incense
and	and	and
Wafers	Triangle	Red Lamp

Water Cup and Wine

West

Much of this will be self-explanatory. A rose or any other fresh flower obtainable from your garden, or elsewhere, is placed in the East – attributed to the element of Air. In the South, together with incense and the fire wand, is a small red lamp, consisting of a small votary candle in a red glass container. Adjacent to the water cup is a small goblet of wine, any wine, preferably a grape wine. At the conclusion of the ceremony, the empty goblet will be inverted to be placed between the Cross and Triangle. In the North, together with the pantacle, instead of the customary crumbs of bread and grains of salt, place a few communion wafers, depending on how many people will be served. These can be obtained from any church supply house, and are ideal for this purpose. On the other hand, if not readily obtainable, fall back simply on a few little bits of bread.

After the Adoration, item No. 25, let the Student stand at the West of Altar, facing East, and read the following declaration:

'For Osiris On-Nophris, who is found perfect before the Gods, hath said: *(Pointing towards the altar)*

These are the elements of my Body
Perfected through Suffering, Glorified through Trial.
For the scent of the dying Rose is as the repressed Sigh of my suffering;
And the flame-red Fire as the Energy of mine Undaunted Will;
And the Cup of Wine is the pouring out of the Blood of my Heart;
Sacrificed unto Regeneration, unto the Newer Life;
And the Bread and Salt are as the foundations of my Body,
Which I destroy in order that they may be renewed.
For I am Osiris Triumphant, even Osiris On-Nophris, the Justified.
I am He who is clothed with the Body of Flesh,
Yet in whom is the Spirit of the Great Gods.
I am the Lord of Life, triumphant over death.
He who partaketh with me shall arise with me;
I am the manifestor in matter of Those whose abode is in the Invisible.
I am purified; I stand upon the Universe.
I am its Reconciler with the Eternal Gods;
I am the Perfector of Matter;
And without Me, the Universe is not.'

As the student passes from the Altar, clockwise, to the East, let him assert:

'I come in the Power of the Light.
I come in the Mercy of the Light.
I come in the Light of Wisdom.
The Light hath healing in its Wings.'

On arriving at the East, stand facing the Air Tablet, extend the arms laterally in the form of a Cross, and say:

'Blessed be Thou, Lord of the Universe, for Thy Glory flows out to the ends of the Universe, rejoicing!'

Drop the arms to the side, and then extend both towards the Air Tablet, with:

'I invite you, all you Beings of the great Eastern Quadrangle – Archangels, Angels, Kings, Rulers and elementals – now assembled in this Temple, to partake with me of the Eucharist of the Four Elements.'

Drop the arms, and move clockwise to the Fire Tablet, extending the arms as above, saying:

'Blessed be Thou, Lord of the Universe, for Thy Glory flows out to the ends of the Universe, rejoicing!'

Then extend both arms towards the Fire Tablet, with:

'I invite you, all you Beings of the great Southern Quadrangle – Archangels, Angels, Kings, Rulers and elementals – now assembled in this Temple, to partake with me of the Eucharist of the Four Elements.'

Drop the arms, move clockwise to the Water Tablet, extending the arms to form a cross, saying:

'Blessed be Thou, Lord of the Universe, for Thy Glory flows out to the ends of the Universe, rejoicing.'

Then extend both arms towards the Water Tablet, with:

'I invite you, all you Beings of the great Western Quadrangle –

Archangels, Angels, Kings, Rulers and elements – now assembled in this Temple, to partake with me of the Eucharist of the Four Elements.'

Drop the arms, move clockwise to the Earth Tablet, extending the arms to form a cross, saying:

'Blessed be Thou, Lord of the Universe, for Thy Glory flows out to the ends of the Universe, rejoicing.'

Then extend both arms towards the Earth Tablet, with:

'I invite you, all you Beings of the great Northern Quadrangle – Archangels, Angels, Kings, Rulers and elementals – now assembled in this Temple, to partake with me of the Eucharist of the Four Elements.'

From the North, he now circumambulates to the East, and from there passes to the West of the Altar facing East. There he makes the projecting Sign, but not the Sign of Silence, and proceeds with the form of the Eucharist.

(*Picking up rose:*) 'I invite you to inhale with me the perfume of this Rose, as a symbol of Air. (*Smells rose.*)

To feel with me the warmth of this sacred lamp, as a symbol of Fire. (*Spreads his hands over it.*)

To eat with me this Bread and Salt (*or Wafer, as the case may be*) as types of Earth. (*Dips bread in salt and eats – or eats wafer.*)

And finally to drink with me this Wine, the consecrated emblem of elemental Water. (*Makes a Cross with the Cup, and then drinks.*)

He then returns the goblet to its place alongside the Water Cup, and passes Clockwise to the East of the Altar facing West.

If a companion is present, he will pass to the West of the Altar vacated by the student, making the projecting Sign but not the sign of silence. The student then replies with the sign of silence and hands the elements to his companion in the same order as above. This is repeated depending on how many communicants are present.

If there are none, then the student-operator goes through the entire process as if addressing a representative of each Elemental Hierarchy.

When these four servings are at an end, he passes to the West of the Altar facing East, takes the wine goblet, drains the last drop of wine, makes the sign of the Cross with the Goblet and, inverting it, places it between the Cross and Triangle in the centre of the Altar, and says:

TETELESTAI!

Depending on how he feels, he may either conclude the ritual immediately, or stand for a while trying to feel the living forces about him.

In order to close the Temple, he asserts:

'Depart in peace unto your abodes and habitations, and let there ever be grace and harmony between us. May the blessing of YEHESHUAH YEHOVASHAH be with you and upon you, now and forevermore. *(Pause.)* I now declare this Temple closed.'

CHAPTER VII

Equipment and Paraphernalia

Having integrated all these diverse segments of ritual into what now appears to me to be a coherent whole, it might not be amiss to deal with a few procedural matters.

If the student has been following the ritual activity from a practical point of view, he might be ready to gradually introduce segments of the paraphernalia and equipment commonly used in ceremonial work.

He might copy the Enochian Tablets on large boards, some twelve by sixteen inches or so. Full instruction as to words, names and colour will be found in Robert Wang's *The Secret Temple*, already mentioned.

The next most significant item to be added would be the altar. A black, wooden, double-cubed affair, either with an opening like a cupboard at the side for storing equipment, or just a plain double cube. It could be covered with a black cloth on which should be placed the emblems of the Golden Dawn, a red cross athwart a white triangle. Around these could be placed the symbols already referred to and briefly described. If you are a Thelemite, the Stele of Revealing could be used instead of cross and triangle.

A collar to hold the lamen could be made of white cloth. If you cannot make it yourself, use a white cord (commonly used for wrapping gifts), or else hire the services of a seamstress to make it for you. Another alternative is to visit a Masonic supply house, and see what supplies they may have which answer your purpose. The simplest lamen or breast plate to be worn is the Hierophant's lamen described in Vol. III of *The Golden Dawn* – a red cross on a green background. This is simple and easy to make, either out of plywood cut with a jig-saw, or from heavy pasteboard. The complete Rose-Cross symbol of the 5=6 grade is admittedly more difficult to make — that is, it is more expensive in terms of both time and effort. But it may well be worth it. For a wand, the simplest one to make is the Hierophant's wand depicted in *The Golden Dawn*. So many of the basic materials required for these items may be found in the nearest hobby shop. It is so much easier to make these things today than ever before; materials are readily available.

If he has already found access to a good seamstress, the student could have a white cotton or nylon gown made, shaped like a T, with gold borders at the hems.

A thurible or censer may be obtained from a church supply shop, or from one of the many stores that have sprung up in recent years catering to the needs of the students interested in modern occultism and wicca.

Anyway, the student can now use his own ingenuity as to his equipment and proceed to operate the ritual as given here in his own way, and according to his own ingenuity.

Relative to the inner working of these rituals, it is too easy to burden the whole subject with far too many complicated instructions. I would prefer to keep them simple at first, and let the student gradually develop his own more complex and perhaps more effectual methods.

The imaginative working of the Pentagram Ritual has been described elsewhere so many times, that it is almost needless to discuss it here. However, in order to ensure that the student does not feel compelled to load himself down with innumerable expensive books, there is included in Appendix Five a short description of the *modus operandi*.

Theoretically, at each of the Cardinal Points, when invoking the Elements before the appropriate Enochian Tablet, the student should assume imaginatively the appropriate Egyptian god-form. These are described in Vol. III of *The Golden Dawn* in the document entitled Z–1. However, these require a good deal of experience and practice to do properly. For the moment these can be ignored or avoided by much more simple expedients.

For example: when invoking the element Air, in the East, the student could imagine himself surrounded by a yellow sphere of light. This will be just as effective as assuming the appropriate god-form, until he feels ready to cope with the latter. In the South, when invoking Fire, he could surround himself with a red fiery sphere. In the West he could use a blue sphere of light; while in the North he could employ a dark green sphere as his auric energy-field. Admittedly these manoeuvres do require some little practice, but they are relatively easy to achieve as compared with the god-forms. And being relatively easy to achieve, the student will *feel* results occurring sooner than otherwise and thus gain enormously in assurance and confidence. This will make it a very short step, as time goes on, and more skill is obtained, to assume the forms of the gods or the Kerubs who rule over the Elements. In other words, one step at a time; begin with the easier practice before proceeding with the complex.

So far as the hexagram ritual is concerned, I have already expressed my total dissatisfaction with the complexity and unnecessary multiplication of figures that are commonly used. Many years ago Crowly devised a unicursal hexagram that can be traced in a single line, rather like a pentagram. The attributions to the unicursal hexagram would be exactly those of the conventional hexagrams. I do not recall anyone having made mention of using this unicursal hexagram in the hexagram ritual. Instruction in its use means showing the direction of movement in both banishing and invoking in relationship to the angle to which a particular planet is attributed. In the Appendix is given this series of attributions which I have found to be just as satisfactory as the conventional hexagram – which means just as easy to use and equally efficacious. I hope that fellow-students will experiment with it and if finding it as satisfactory as I have, to let me know so that further record can be made of this matter.

I am also taking the liberty of attaching, as a second part to this book, a monogram I wrote many years ago on The Bornless Ritual. I am including it here mainly because there are an enormous number of resemblances between the Opening by Watchtower and the Bornless Ritual. The major difference is that in the Bornless Ritual there are a large number of so-called barbarous names of evocation.

These, of course, are lacking in the Opening by Watchtower.

My prime motive, however, for including it here, is so that the student can make a comparison between the two rituals and perceive the enormous resemblances that exist between them. This may, in turn, help the student to appreciate the point of view I have long taken, that Crowley is best understood in the light of his former connection with The Golden Dawn.

Beyond all these explanations however, it should demonstrate the method by means of which rituals are elaborated or constructed from simple elements. It is this understanding which is of prime importance, and should stand the student in good stead in the future. For then he will be able to stand on his own two feet, and not rely on anyone else for help in ritual construction. His own methods, no matter how simple or naive, are infinitely to be preferred to someone else's, however more accurate and poetic and complete they may appear to be.

PART TWO

CHAPTER VIII

Background Data

The Bornless Ritual first saw the light of day and received a slight degree of public notice when Mr Charles W. Goodwin, M.A., a member of the Cambridge Antiquarian Society, published in 1852 a monogram entitled *A Fragment of a Graeco-Egyptian Ritual*. It gave both the Greek text with an English translation accompanied by a few erudite but not very literary notes (Appendix One).

Later, towards the close of the nineteenth century, part of this same archaic ritual was reproduced in a slim volume entitled *Egyptian Magic* by E. A. Wallis Budge, one-time Keeper of Antiquities in the British Museum.

The only other and much later reference to it is to be found as the Preliminary Invocation in a book entitled *The Goetia – The Lesser Key of King Solomon* (Appendix Three). Commissioned and paid for by Aleister Crowley while he was still a member of the Hermetic Order of the Golden Dawn, it had been translated from the Latin by S. L. MacGregor Mathers in the opening years of the twentieth century. Mathers previously had translated and published *The Greater Key of King Solomon*, a larger and better known book of talismans and incantations. Crowley's *Goetia* was published in a handsome deluxe edition, so typical of Crowley, around the year 1903, with an introduction denouncing MacGregor Mathers. The Preliminary Invocation was printed in heavy Gothic type. I doubt if it attracted much attention, save from pirate-publishers. One of them, located in Chicago, republished it several years later, in a cheap American edition.

Early in the 1920s, while in Cefalu, Sicily, Aleister Crowley took his original Preliminary Invocation, and based upon some twenty years of active work with it, edited it, vastly expanding it with a protracted and most illuminating commentary (Appendix Three). It appeared later in his book *Magick, In Theory and Practice*.

The simple form of the Preliminary Invocation from *The Goetia* was also utilized in my book *The Tree of Life*. Again, after my stint in the Order of the Golden Dawn, I republished it in the original edition of *The Golden Dawn*. However, this latter version was very similar to Crowley's version in *Magick*, minus however the phallic over-emphasis and the sometimes (as I once thought) ludicrous interpretation of the 'barbarous names of evocation'. Instead it did include several Order invocations or prayers and other ritualistic procedures that I had learned while in the Order. It is not included in this book; it is too cumbersome.

After Goodwin's publication of the crude form of this archaic ritual, it must have been quietly and secretly taken over by certain Adepti of the Golden Dawn interested in Egyptology. Several members must have been deeply involved in this subject, for a few books have been written attempting to prove that the Egyptian *Book of the Dead*, so called, was not merely a collection of funerary spells but, in effect, comprised part of an initiatory magical ritual.

For example, there is *The Ritual of the Mystery of the Soul* by M. W. Blackden, S.R.I.A., VII° (Bernard Quaritch, London, no date). We learn from Arthur E. Waite's biography that Blackden was a member not only of the Societas Rosicruciana in Anglia but of the Golden Dawn as well, and indeed was one of the three who governed the Order after the fateful Revolt of 1900.

Then there is *The Book of the Master of the Hidden Places*, by W. Marsham Adams (John Murray, London, 1885 reprinted by The Aquarian Press, 1980). Marsham's book contains many references to Freemasonry. It would seem that he was attempting, among other things, to relate modern Masonic teaching to an esoteric interpretation of *The Book of the Dead*. In the year 1933, this book reappeared with an introduction and edited by E.J. Langford Garstin (Search Publishing Co. London, 1933). Garstin was also a member of the Golden Dawn, and in fact a former chief of one of the now independent factions.

These items are mentioned solely as background material to substantiate the idea that the elaboration of the Ritual under consideration by members of the Golden Dawn was more than a possibility, though admittedly there is no factual evidence pointing thereto.

In any event, in their hands the primitive ritual underwent considerable modification and literary refinement. Ultimately, most traces of its crude beginnings were eliminated. I say *most*, certainly not all. For this ritual is replete with innumerable so-called barbarous names of evocation whose origin is practically impossible to trace, as well as containing one particular paragraph which is repeated several times:

> Come thou forth and follow me, and make all spirits subject unto me so that every spirit of the firmament and of the ether, upon the earth and under the earth, on dry land and in the water, of whirling air and of rushing fire, and every spell and scourge of God may be made obedient unto me.

This is classical magic in the most primitive sense of the word, in which the shaman or magician proposes to compel the animistic forces of nature to be subservient to his wishes.

Budge has something to say about these primitive or barbarous words. For example, in the book previously mentioned, he wrote: 'The last class of documents [i.e. magical papyri used by Gnostics and other sects] undoubtedly contains a very large proportion of the magical ideas, beliefs, formulae, etc., which were current in Egypt from the time of the Ptolemies to the end of the Roman period, but from about 150 B.C. to A.D. 200, the papyri exhibit traces of the influence of Greek, Hebrew, and Syrian philosophers and magicians, and from a passage like the following, we may get a proof of this.'

At this point, Budge quotes the Bornless Ritual at length, using of course the Goodwin version. In this passage, he goes on to write: 'Osoronnophris is clearly a corruption of the old Egyptian names of the great god of the dead "Anser Unnefer", and Paphro seems to represent the Egyptian Per-āa (literally "great house") or

"Pharoah", with the article *pa*, "the", prefixed. It is interesting to note that Moses is mentioned, a fact which seems to indicate Jewish influence.'

Apparently the earliest English renditions of this Graeco-Egyptian ritual do not contain the long lists of barbarous names of evocation, though they are to be seen in the Greek version; Goodwin did not transliterate them. Neither did Wallis Budge give an account of them. What their origins are remain to this day altogether obscure.

What they mean is also anybody's guess. It is quite true that a few can be analyzed and found to be corruptions of divine names in the Egyptian, Greek and Hebrew tongues. For instance, *Sabao* is thought to be a corruption of the Hebrew *Tzabaoth* meaning 'hosts', commonly coupled either with Elohim or Tetragrammaton.

Abrasar is quite evidently derived from the old Gnostic deity name 'Abraxas' or 'Abrasax', often represented in a form which has a human body, the head of a hawk or cock, and legs terminating in serpents. There is little doubt that he was a form of the Sun god, and that he was intended to represent some aspect of the Creator of the world. 'The name was believed to possess magical powers of the highest class, and Basileides who gave it currency in the second century, seems to have regarded it as an invincible name.'

IAO was intended to represent one of the Hebrew names for Almighty God, 'Jah', says Wallis Budge also. Furthermore, the names 'Adonai, Eloai' are derived through the Hebrew from the Bible. Some of the remaining names could be explained by Hebrew and Syriac words.

But others are not thus to be derived at all, so unrecognizable and distorted have they become. In Aleister Crowley's analysis of the barbarous names, he has followed only his own sexual inclinations, which is perhaps as it should be. The only difficulty is that some of the interpretations or analyses, while basically correct and rooted in Yetziratic tradition, sound ludicrous at first and echo only his own personal sexual proclivities.

In the 'Interlude' of Part II of *Book 4*, which the publisher unfortunately omitted from the first Sangreal edition, Crowley has indulged his Qabalistic erudition and rich sense of humour in the interpretation of some traditional nursery rhymes. The result is extraordinarily illuminating, apart from his satire and humour. It indicates simply that the more profound knowledge one brings to the task, the more intelligible becomes even rank nonsense.

It therefore seems evident that much the same is true in applying this theme to the string of names to be found as parts of the Bornless Ritual. Some of these names Crowley has quite successfully fitted into the framework of his own Thelemic philosophy and theology. Others are equally evidently tortured to suit his own particular views on the relationship of sex and religion – in other words, to suit his version of a solar-phallic religion predicated on *The Book of the Law*.

Yet, piling up here and there is evidence tending to validate much of what Crowley essayed years ago, to lend credibility to some of his seemingly grotesque interpretations. For many years, though I could manage to follow the Qabalistic principles involved in his arbitrary rendering of the barbarous names employed in this ritual, I constantly felt almost outraged, or put upon, as it were, when reading them. Somehow I felt they were excessive, or perhaps unnecessary.

In recent years, however, much has occurred to cause me to modify the above reaction. For example, I recommend to the student with an eye for research a book entitled *The Sacred Mushroom and the Cross* by John M. Allegro. The author is a lecturer in Old Testament and inter-testamental studies at a leading English University. His previous book *The Dead Sea Scrolls* (Penguin edition, 1964) should be required reading for every serious student of the Mysteries. The Introduction, a masterly piece of work, to the first-mentioned book, read in conjunction with Crowley's interpretations of the barbarous names, leads one immediately to the conclusion that no matter how fanciful they seem to be at first sight, there may be considerable philological and not merely symbolic justification for them. Regardless of whether or not Mr Allegro's particular thesis is substantiated by other scholars, nonetheless his present contribution provides another linguistic key which helps turn the rusty lock to give fundamental meaning to these ancient and obscure words.

It would not be too difficult for any writer with a workable knowledge of the intricacies of Qabalistic manipulation to give value and substance of some kind to these words. *Gematria* and *Notariqon* are exquisitely sensitive tools – or bludgeons, as the case may be – to convert these meaningless words into profoundly significant proofs of his understanding of Qabalistic philosophy. Even forty years ago, when writing *The Garden of Pomegranates*, I demonstrated quite clearly and simply that these tools could be used to extract meaning from some otherwise hard nuts that other writers had barely managed to crack.

However, I do not think that this is required of the student or aspirant who would use this Ritual as an aid to acquire a higher state of consciousness. The mere fact that he is, first of all, aspiring, is enough to render these words effective. Their very unintelligibility is sufficient, given the right circumstances, to exalt consciousness beyond its ordinary limits and boundaries. They thus serve as stimulants to transcend the boundaries of our everyday prosaic awareness. They are intoxicants or psychedelic aids. As such they need to be used with enormous care – but they may be used nonetheless.

CHAPTER IX
Concerning the Bornless Ritual

It is quite probable that Allan Bennett, whose Order sacramental name was G. H. Frater Yehi Aour ('Let there be light'), first introduced this ritual to Aleister Crowley. After the latter joined the Order in 1898, he met Allan Bennett who was sick and poverty-stricken at the time. Crowley made the magnanimous gesture of offering Allan the use of his flat in London. The two men shared the apartment, and under these close circumstances, Allan taught Crowley the intricacies of the Qabalah and the complex principles of ritual magic.

From this moment forward, the Bornless Ritual became Crowley's personal ritual. It now becomes wholly impossible to discuss the Ritual itself without bringing Crowley into consideration. As previously remarked, he had first published it in *The Goetia*. This was one of his early gestures of defiance of MacGregor Mathers and the Golden Dawn, which was then in a state of collapse following the Revolt of 1900. Years later, after his own spiritual attainment, Crowley edited it, critically but sympathetically, expanding it into a considerable document entitled *Liber Samekh*.

As an aside, and to demonstrate the associative processes involved in Crowley's thinking, it should be noted that the Hebrew letter *Samekh* is attributed to that Path on the Tree of Life linking *Yesod* to *Tiphareth*. One of its several other attributions is Sagittarius, the Path of the Arrow, representing of course aspiration to the higher. Thus the Ritual has become identified with the means of aspiring towards and attaining the Knowledge and Conversation of the Holy Guardian Angel.

At this juncture a number of definitions are in order so that what follows may be clarified.

The phrase 'The Holy Guardian Angel' is extrapolated from *The Sacred Magic of Abramelin the Mage*, another text which was translated from the French by MacGregor Mathers. The author of this book is supposed to have been one Abraham, who acknowledged the receipt of the magical system described in the book from an Egyptian named Abramelin. There is doubtless mythology involved here. Regardless of its origin, its date and its authorship, however, this work was found to be of value to some of the adepts of the Golden Dawn and many other students, as already indicated. The author makes no impossible demands such as are found in the fraudulent grimoires concerning the blood of bats caught at midnight, or the fourth feather from the left wing of a completely black cock, or the stuffed eye of a virgin basilisk, and so on.

Though perhaps some of the requirements are difficult to follow, there is always an excellent reason for their statement: they are not intended to be subtle tests of the skill of the operator. Certain preliminary prescriptions and injunctions need to be observed. But these really amount to little more than commonsense counsel, to observe decency in the performance of so august an operation.

For example, one should possess a house where proper precautions against disturbance and interference can be taken. This having been arranged, there remains little else to do but aspire, with increasing concentration and ardour, for six months towards the Knowledge and Conversation of the Holy Guardian Angel.

This latter phrase which was wholeheartedly adopted by Aleister Crowley, was synonymous with the Golden Dawn reference to the Higher Genius and the Theosophical term the Higher Self. There is a reference in Equinox I, p. 159, written by Crowley, which is worth quoting in this connection:

> Lytton calls him Adonai in *Zanoni*, and I often use this name in the note-books.
> Abramelin calls him Holy Guardian Angel. I adopt this:
> 1. Because system is so simple and effective. 2. Because since *all* theories of the universe are absurd, it is better to talk in the language of one which is patently absurd, so as to mortify the metaphysical man ...

The Golden Dawn calls him the Genius. Gnostics say the Logos.
Egyptians say Asar Un-Nefer ...
We also get metaphysical analyses of His nature, deeper and deeper
according to the subtlety of the writer; for this vision – it is all one same
phenomenon, variously coloured by our varying Ruachs – is, I believe,
the first and last of all spiritual experience.

In a Golden Dawn manuscript entitled *The Microcosm*, the Holy
Guardian Angel or the Genius is lengthily but adequately defined in
Qabalistic terms as follows:

> This spiritual consciousness *(Daath)* is the focus of the action of
> *Neschamah*. The spiritual consciousness is, in its turn, the Throne or
> Vehicle of the Life of the Spirit which is *Chiah*; and these combined
> form the Chariot of that Higher Will which is in *Kether*. Also it is the
> peculiar faculty of *Neschamah* to aspire unto that which is beyond. The
> Higher Will manifests itself through *Yechidah* ... The Shining Flame of
> the Divine Fire, the *Kether* of the Body, is the Real Self of the
> Incarnation ... This *Yechidah* is the only part of the man which can truly
> say *EHEIEH*, I am. This is then but the *Kether* of the *Assiah* of the
> Microcosm, that is, it is the highest part of man as Man ... Behind
> *Yechidah* are Angelic and Archangelic Forces of which *Yechidah* is the
> manifestor. It is therefore the Lower Genius or Viceroy of the Higher
> Genius which is beyond, an Angel Mighty and Terrible. This Great
> Angel is the Higher Genius, beyond which are the Archangelic and
> Divine.

Though Crowley constantly shifted emphasis of meaning relative
to the Holy Guardian Angel, it should be noted that throughout his
commentary to *The Book of the Law*, recently published as *The Law
is For All*, there is no equivocation whatsoever. The Higher Self *is*
the Holy Guardian Angel – and that is that. No ambiguity is there,
no straining of interpretation. It is a clear statement of fact.

The Ritual opens up with an invocation: 'Thee I invoke the
Bornless One.' One of Crowley's most harsh and virulent critics
once attempted to ridicule all modern interpretations of magic, after
referring to Goodwin's original text, by stating that the more
accurate translation should have been 'The Headless One'. The
Greek word in the text is *acephalon*. *Cephalon* is the Greek root from
which many anatomical terms have been derived. Thus: *cephalon* –

the brain. *Rhinencephalon* – the old nose brain. *Mesencephalon* – the midbrain. Encephalitis, of course, is another derivative with 'itis' (inflammation) added as a suffix.

Cephalon, then, means 'head'. The prefix is the privative article 'a', meaning *not, without*, etc., as in agnostic, atheist, analgesic, etc. *Cephalon* with the prefix then means 'without a head', or 'headless'.

In many primitive languages, the word 'head' is often used as an equivalent of 'beginning' – as for example in the Hebrew 'Rosh ha-Shanah'. Literally this means the 'head of the year'. It is idiomatic for the beginning of the year, or the New Year. So 'the Headless One' or the 'Beginningless One' is of course the Eternal One, the One without a beginning, the Bornless One. It rather reminds me of a few lines from Sir Edwin Arnold's *Song Celestial*:

> Never the spirit was born,
> The Spirit shall cease to be never.
> Never was time it was not,
> End and beginning are dreams.
> Birthless and deathless and changeless
> Remaineth the Spirit for ever,
> Death hath not touched it at all,
> Dead though the house of it seems.

While on this topic of the Abramelin method and the term the Holy Guardian Angel, I should mention that throughout the years many students have reported to me some of their efforts and experiences in this direction. Almost without exception, all have failed, their sincerity notwithstanding. They retired from the world for six months, following either the literal dictates of the book, or else Crowley's recommendation for the use of the Bornless Ritual:

> Let the Adept perform this Ritual aright, perfect in every part thereof, once daily for one moon, then twice, at dawn and dusk, for two moons, next thrice, noon added, for three moons. Afterwards, midnight, making up his course, for four moons four times every day. Then let the eleventh Moon be consecrated wholly to this Work; let him be instant in continual ardour, dismissing all but his sheer needs to eat and sleep.

Most failed, despite effort and devotion. Some few then turned their backs on the whole subject, and spewed their frustration and futility on all who came within their sphere. A few others, on the basis of this failure, began to ask 'Why?'.

There is no easy answer to this question. So many factors require consideration. Yet, when all is said and done, there is one requirement which only a handful of people seem to perceive. That is, the need for a preliminary period of inner discipline of one kind or another. It is this arduous training which then comes to the aid of the aspirant during the six months term of his retirement, making possible or feasible the ultimate attainment.

Discipline as a rule is not welcome among occult students, which was why Crowley insisted so emphatically upon its necessity, and why he tended to be rude and contemptuous when students sought the highest goals without proper preparation. It seems to me, then, that when aspirants attempt to perform the Abramelin operation in the six months or eleven month period recommended, and fail to observe any preparatory mental or magical discipline, their aspiration needs to be held suspect. I rather fancy many of them are neurotic escapists who cannot tolerate themselves or their emotional difficulties. They hope and fantasize that the Abramelin operation will 'cure' them of their inner problems, which will thus not have to be faced.

Escape is no part of the Great Work – failure can only ensue. Discipline and training, the traditional requirements in magic as well as elsewhere, are the only factors that can ensure success. There is no other way.

It seems to me therefore that the regimen needs to be rationally modified in terms of the capacity and ability of each student. Instead of trying to rush results, he would do better to devote himself steadfastly to the discipline, working assiduously at his appointed tasks, using the ritual described in this book once daily, or more often as he has the skill and time to perform, without imposing on himself a time limit. In this way, he could work quietly but steadily over a long period of time, perhaps several years, until the illumination dawns upon him when he is ready, in God's own good time.

Crowley's version of this ritual – and presumably the Golden Dawn attitude, as expressed in its own Ritual for the invocation of the Higher Self – demands but a single celebrant. This is the student or aspirant who for months at a time, or better still throughout his whole lifetime, aspires towards the Holy Guardian Angel to become its vehicle and agent. There is another version, derivative from a former student of Crowley's, but I doubt one that met with the approval of Crowley. It employs the component parts of the ritual, even as Crowley had split it up, but delivers each component part into the hands of a different celebrant. In this way it becomes transformed into a group ritual, a dramatic ritual in which a group of aspirants participate. Each contributes his own energy, his own emotions and feelings, and his own aspiration to the ceremony – in his own way. And just as in group therapy, the emotional response of any one participant may affect or precipitate a similar emotional crisis in another fellow-member, so in the multiple-celebrant ritual, any one aspirant's attainment may spread, contagion-like, to the others, like a spark setting fire to adjacent dry kindle, to create a conflagration.

It can, unfortunately, get very close to hysteria – as in the products of a revival meeting under a tent; but at the same time it is quite possible, all other things being equal, that in a group which has been specially selected as having been prepared both by life and training, the fire of enlightenment could readily be communicated from one to another in the group working.

CHAPTER X

Original Intent of the Bornless Ritual

The original contents of this ritual, while obscure historically, are patently coarse, crude, rudimentary and elemental, and very distant from the modern spiritual interpretation that many of us have become used to. It represents an excellent example of what Jung called *enantiodromia*, a conversion from one point of view to its direct opposite.

The original simple intention of this ritual was exorcism, to cast out a demon from a possessed person. In the words of Goodwin's original: 'Hear me and drive away this spirit. I call thee the terrible and invisible god residing in the empty wind ... thou headless one, deliver such an one from the spirit that possesses him ...'

The modern intent of this ritual as developed within the Order of the Golden Dawn and eventually by Aleister Crowley is, quite remarkably, the exact opposite. The purpose of the ritual, as we have already seen, is so to open the mind of the aspirant by continuous and concentrated application, that he becomes conscious of – or, if you like, possessed by – another spirit, the Holy Guardian Angel. This we have already defined. But this is a very far cry from the intent of the original ritual as translated by Goodwin over a century ago.

After having been appropriated by Allan Bennett and others, the ritual was intended to be operated in a Golden Dawn Temple set up for the Neophyte Grade. In a document labelled Z–1 which analyzed in fine detail every ritual-gesture and every temple movement of both officer and candidate, the temple itself is described as a microcosm of the macrocosm, patterned on the Tree of Life, which is the basis for all Qabalistic thinking and working:

Of the Temple in reference to the Sephiroth. The Temple, as arranged in the Neophyte Grade of the Order of the Golden Dawn in the Outer, is placed looking towards the YH of YHVH in *Malkuth* in *Assiah.* That is, as Y and H answer unto the Sephiroth *Chokmah* and *Binah* on the Tree (and unto *Abba* and *Aimah,* through whose knowledge alone that of *Kether* may be obtained), even so, the sacred rites of the Temple may gradually, and as it were, in spite of himself, lead the Neophyte unto the knowledge of his Higher Self.

In other words – to cut through the technicality of these Qabalistic clichés – the East of the temple is so arranged as to point directly towards the supernal Sephiroth.

The far East is, as it were, the direction of *Kether,* the Crown, the highest Sephirah on the Tree. As such it also represents the Lower Genius which is the Throne or vehicle of the Higher Genius of the more subtle Qabalistic worlds.

The Temple, thus arranged, is formally opened as in the Neophyte Ceremony (see *The Golden Dawn,* Vol. II, p. 12). That is to say, it is consecrated with fire and water after a preliminary ceremonial banishing, so as to maintain a clear and pure area where the aspirant will not be disturbed or contaminated by alien intrusion.

Then follows the Adoration, which is a remnant of an old Gnostic prayer. This has the effect of placing the aspirant under divine guidance, and while so guided he declares in a well-defined statement what the intention of the ceremony is. This does not appear in full clarity in *Liber Samekh* itself. However, insofar as the latter has been adapted from fundamental Golden Dawn procedures, as proven by intrinsic evidence, it must logically follow, since this was certainly one of its most important precepts. Any ceremonial must declare, after the adoration and circumambulation, the purpose and intent of the ritual to follow, as though thereby the intent is sanctified and clarified.

The invocation itself follows. Its opening stanza enumerates the characteristics or qualities of this eternal Spirit, the Holy Guardian Angel. It is as though by enumerating these, the aspirant may ultimately become conscious of what actually he is. It implies that by the reiteration of *tat tvam asi* – with prolonged meditation upon its meaning of 'that thou art' – the realization may dawn within the conscious ego of the indwelling or overshadowing Self. Repetition and suggestion, plus the exaltation of consciousness that accompany the use of ceremonial ritual, may indeed eventuate in a true mystical or psychedelic experience or expansion of consciousness to include the awareness of the fact that one is and always has been the Bornless Spirit.

A further word is required here relative to the Holy Guardian Angel. It is true that earlier I have related this to the higher and divine Genius of the Golden Dawn and to the Higher Self of the Theosophists. I do not wish to labour the reality of the mystical or transcendental experience. This has already been established elsewhere and by other people. For the Jungians, it is an established fact pertinent to their own system. And there is a new school of psychologists in process of development. They regard the mystical experience as a healthy development in the onward growth of the psyche. They do not consider this phenomenon outside of their psychological field, as did some nineteenth century scientists. Since it is a naturalistic piece of human behaviour, it is regarded as well within their scientific purview, rather than as belonging to the field of religion. Instead of the familiar phrase the 'religious' or 'mystical' experience, they have coined a new phrase, the 'peak' experience to refer to the same inner phenomenon. They are inclined to view its occurrence as a good deal more common than was previously supposed, and that there is a spontaneity in its frequency. (See my *Roll Away the Stone.*)

It needs to be mentioned here that as a result of intense concentration, prayer or invocation 'the conditions of thought, time and space are abolished'. It is impossible to explain what this really means; only experience can furnish you with comprehension.

A further development is the appearance of the Form which has been universally described as human; although the persons describing it proceed to add a great number of details which are not human at all. This particular appearance is usually assumed to be 'God'.

Whatever it may be, the result on the mind is tremendous; all his thoughts are pushed to their greatest development. He sincerely believes that they have the divine sanction; perhaps he even supposes

that they emanate from this 'God'. He goes back into the world armed
with this intense conviction and authority. He proclaims his ideas
without the restraint which is imposed upon most persons by doubt,
modesty and diffidence; while further there is, one may suppose, a real
clarification.*

In other words, whatever the contents of the unconscious psyche
may be, they become wholly inundated with a tremendous flow of
energy. They thus become inflamed and activated. For the
Christian, this 'form' will therefore appear to be Jesus of Nazareth
or Mary, or anybody else in the Christian pantheon. For the
Mohammedan, he will be the Prophet or the Angel Gabriel who
brought the message to Mohammed. The Buddhist devotee likewise
will see Sakya Muni, and so forth.

However, so far as I am aware, it is only the Buddhist canon
which provides adequate warnings against taking these visions at
their face value. Its basic theme is that the forgotten or repressed
residues of the mind become activated by intense concentration or
emotional fervour, so that when illumination does occur, these
residues take on practically substantial form.

In *The Tibetan Book of the Dead*, where the officiating lama is
described as directing the attention of the newly-deceased through
the Bardo or Underworld, the lama continually affirms the fact that
both the beneficent and wrathful deities are, in effect, only thought-
forms which must be perceived as such. If not, the deceased person
loses the immediate opportunity to experience the Clear Light and
thus to achieve liberation.

Since this is rooted in the Mahayana metaphysic, it is also to be
presumed that the lama-guru impresses upon the novitiate that the
apparently divine 'Form' which appears during meditation or the
tantric rites is not only symbolic of the all-transcendent Bodhi but
that it includes and is also contaminated, as it were, by the repressed
infantile images based on early sectarian religious training, dormant
in the psyche throughout the life-time.

Thus, to return to our Bornless Ritual, the form which the Holy
Guardian Angel assumes must differ for each aspirant who proceeds

* Aleister Crowley, *Book 4*, Part 1.

with this particular discipline. No two students will experience identically the mystical event, nor will they perceive the same Form – though each will know that this Form is his Holy Guardian Angel, which has already been defined as the mediator or the link between the aspirant and the Unknown Glory beyond.

Two things beyond all others are demanded of the aspirant in holy discipline. First, that he examine scrupulously, with the aid of his superior if he has one, the contents of his transcendental experience – after the ecstasy and emotional storm have subsided. Without in any way denying the validity of the enlightenment itself, he must thoroughly analyze both its form and content. In this manner, the unconscious residuals or archetypes may be perceived for what they are and so separated from the essential illumination itself.

The other alternative – and this need not be opposed to the previous recommendation – is to embark upon a course of psychotherapy in the years prior to embarking upon so crucial an experiment as the Holy Guardian operation. It is like pouring a fine wine into an unwashed bottle if one 'works for enlightenment' without clarifying the psychic vehicle through which the enlightenment can occur. The mind must be prepared thoroughly for the most devastating and the most rewarding experience of the life-time. As such, the most minute, painstaking and thorough-going preparation needs to be taken. No half-measures will suffice – or else one winds up as a complete fanatic or a mere 'nut', depending on what lies fallow within the psyche.

CHAPTER XI

Comparisons

The Preliminary Invocation as published in *The Goetia* in 1903 set the ground for the later more complex elaborations developed by Crowley in Cefalu. The ritual is split up into several component parts, headed by Hebrew letters. These would be most meaningful to the Golden Dawn initiate or any student of the Qabalah, as representing simple attributions from the *Sepher Yetzirah*, one of the most archaic of the Qabalistic texts. Thus *Aleph*, the first subdivision, would represent the element Air. *Shin*, the second, would represent the element Fire. (Sometimes *Shin* is called upon for double service, since it may also represent Spirit.) *Mem*, the third of the so-called 'three Mother letters', would represent Water, while *Tau*, basically representing Saturn in the Path system of the Tree, has to do double duty in being attributed to the element Earth. To this extent it is remarkably akin to the ritual described in this work.

There is a further subdivision headed by the word *Amen*, which in this context is made to represent the fifth Element Spirit. Since in the Golden Dawn concepts, Spirit has both a positive and a negative phase, this section of the ritual has two parts.

Actually it has three, as will be perceived by referring to Appendix Four. Crowley wiggles off the dilemma neatly by attributing two sections to one pole, and a single section to the other. It is arbitrary of course, but permissible.

In the original, the finale of the Ritual commencing 'I am He, the Bornless Spirit' is not attributed to anything, but in *Liber Samekh*, Crowley entitles it correctly the Attainment without giving it a symbol. By intent and implication, it presents the picture of the aspirant, no longer invoking the Bornless Spirit, but now affirming his identity with it. He has attained.

The opening of the ritual reiterates that the play of the opposites – night and day, the earth and the heavens, light and darkness, male and the female, the seed and the fruit, the moist and the dry, etc. – are the work of the Angel. It is only through these polarities that he is able to operate in his task of obtaining experience of any and every kind through his vehicle. But it is essential to note the repeated affirmation that these opposites are created by the Self, which is divinity.

In this connection, it is worth remembering that tremendously significant sentence in Sir Edwin Arnold's version of the *Bhagavad Gita*: 'I who am all, made it all, and abide its separate Lord.' It is the last clause which the Ritual emphasizes – the Angel is wholly apart from his own creation. He is immanent as well as transcendent.

Man may construct a dream in the night, feel that the dream indeed is himself in action, expresses himself and his deepest needs and wishes; yet as the maker of the dream, he is altogether apart from it. He is the dreamer.

This is the intrinsic message of the proem, or Oath as Crowley chooses to call it. It says he is Asar Un-Nefer – Man made perfect. Another part of the Golden Dawn material asserts of Osiris: 'This is my body which I destroy in order that it may be renewed.' The corollary also is that this is my body which I renew in order that it may be destroyed. The magical ritual makes no attempt to evade issues by stating half-way measures. It gives the Truth.

It even has the Angel stating: 'I am He, the Truth!'

It is up to the aspirant to grasp this truth through exaltation and the expansion of consciousness. Only in this way can the opposites be transcended, united, and in fact utilized. The Eastern notion of *nirdvandva*, of detachment, is hardly applicable to the Western man deeply involved in all the everyday problems that develop during the process of extracting the uttermost from his present incarnation. But once he has grasped the idea that the opposites are in effect his own creation – the dynamic play of the forces of which he is composed – then he can proceed with the involvement and do that which he knows needs to be done. All the time, he will know full well that this is the particular game he is playing and so of course is detached. It is as though, while playing chess, one is bound by quite arbitrary rules governing the movement of the pieces on the board. Yet one can either enjoy the game, being bound by the rules, or at a moment's notice sweep all the pieces off the board, and walk away knowing that none of this has anything to do with what one essentially is.

The appreciation of these fundamental facts or concepts explode the idiotic fantasy that a quick run-through of the Ritual will yield illumination, from which the above realization will emerge with clarity and vigour. It is the daily use of the Ritual and/or its equivalent described in Part One over months and years, with prolonged meditation on its meaning which expands with every investigation of the inner world, culminating in the emergence of Life, Light, Love and Liberty. The whole self needs to be transformed by consecrated and dedicated work, devotion to the ideal – and time and effort are merely two of the factors required to achieve these ends. The student who believes he can run away from his life-obligations to a country-house and play at magic by reciting this ritual once or twice per day, is sorely deceiving himself.

Appendix I

FRAGMENT OF A GRAECO-EGYPTIAN WORK UPON MAGIC, FROM A PAPYRUS IN THE BRITISH MUSEUM, EDITED FOR THE CAMBRIDGE ANTIQUARIAN SOCIETY, WITH A TRANSLATION BY CHARLES WYCLIFFE GOODWIN, 1852.

The Greek Text

Στήλη τοῦ Θεοῦ τοῦ ζωγρ. εἰς τὴν ἐπιστολήν.

Σὲ καλῶ, τὸν ἀκέφαλον, τὸν κτίσαντα γῆν καὶ οὐρανὸν, τὸν κτίσαντα νύκτα καὶ ἡμέραν, σὲ τὸν κτίσαντα φῶς καὶ σκότος. Σὺ εἶ Ὀσορόννωφρις, ὃν οὐδεὶς εἶδε πώποτε, σὺ εἶ Ἰαβας, σὺ εἶ Ἰάπως, σὺ διέκρεινας τὸ δίκαιον καὶ τὸ ἄδικον, σὺ ἐποίησας θῆλυ καὶ ἄρρεν, σὺ ἔδειξας σποράν καὶ καρπούς, σὺ ἐποίησας τοὺς ἀνθρώπους ἀλληλοφιλεῖν καὶ ἀλληλομισεῖν. Ἐγώ εἰμι Μούσης ὁ προφήτης σου, ᾧ παρέδωκας τὰ μυστήριά σου τὰ συντελούμενα Ἰστράηλ, σὺ ἔδειξας ὑγρὸν καὶ ξηρὸν καὶ πᾶσαν τροφήν. Ἐπάκουσόν μου· ἐγώ εἰμι ἄγγελος τοῦ Φάπρω Ὀσορόννωφρις, τοῦτό ἐστίν σου τὸ ὄνομα τὸ ἀλήθινον, τὸ παραδιδόμενον τοῖς προφήταις Ἰστράηλ. Ἐπάκουσόν μου, αρ . . . θιαω, ρειβετ, αθελεβερσηθ, α . . βλαθα, αβευ, εβεν, φι, χιτασοη, ιβ . . θιαω, εἰσάκουσόν μου καὶ ἀπόστρεψον τὸ δαιμόνιον τοῦτο. Ἐπικαλοῦμαί σε τὸν ἐν τῷ κενῷ πνεύματι δεινὸν καὶ ἀόρατον θεὸν, αρογογοροβραω, σοχου, μοδοριω, φαλαρχαω, οοο, απε, ἀκέφαλε, ἀπάλλαξον τὸν δεῖνα ἀπὸ τοῦ συνέχοντος αὐτὸν δαίμονος. Ρουβριαω, μαριωδαμ, βαλβναβαωθ, ασσαλωναι, αφνιαω, ι, θωληθ, αβρασαξ, αηοων, ἰσχυρὲ, ἀκέφαλε, ἀπάλλαξον τὸν δεῖνα ἀπὸ τοῦ συνέχοντος αὐτὸν δαί- μονος. Μα, βαρραιω, ιωηλ, κοθα, αθορηβαλω, αβραωθ, ἀπάλλαξον τὸν δεῖνα. Λωθ, αβαωθ, βασυμ, ἰσακ, σαβαωθ, ιαω, οὗτός ἐστιν ὁ κύριος τῶν θεῶν, οὗτός ἐστιν ὁ κύριος τῆς οἰκουμένης, οὗτός ἐστιν ὃν οἱ ἄνεμοι φοβοῦνται, οὗτός ἐστιν ὁ ποιήσας φωνὴν προστάγματι ἑαυτοῦ, πάντων[1] κύριε, βασιλεῦ, δύναστα, βοηθέ, σῶσον ψυχὴν, ιεου, πυρ, ιου, πυρ, ιαωτ, ιαηω, ιοου, αβρασαξ, σαβριαμ, οο, υυ, ευ, οο, υυ, αδωναιε, ηδε, εδυ, ἄγγελος τοῦ θεοῦ, ανλαλα, λαι, γαια, απα, διαχαννα, χορυν, ἐγώ εἰμι ὁ ἀκέφαλος δαίμων ἐν τοῖς ποσὶν ἔχων τὴν ὁρασιν, ἰσχυρὸς, τὸ πῦρ τὸ ἀθάνατον, ἐγώ εἰμι ἡ ἀλήθεια, ὁ μεισῶν ἀδικήματα γείνεσθαι ἐν τῷ κόσμῳ, ἐγώ εἰμι ὁ ἀστράπτων καὶ βροντῶν, ἐγώ εἰμι οὗ ἐστιν ὁ ἱδρως ὄμβρος ἐπιπείπτων ἐπὶ τὴν γῆν ἵνα ὀχεύῃ, ἐγώ εἰμι οὗ τὸ στόμα καίεται δι' ὅλου, ἐγώ εἰμι ὁ γεννῶν καὶ ἀπογεννῶν, ἐγώ εἰμι ἡ χάρις τοῦ αἰῶνος, ὄνομά μοι καρδία περιζωσμένη ὄφιν. Ἔξελθε καὶ ἀκολού- θησον. Τελετὴ τῆς προκειμένης ποιήσεως. Γράψας τὰ ὀνό- ματα εἰς καινὸν χαρτάριον καὶ διατείνας ἀπὸ κροτάφου εἰς κρόταφον σεαυτοῦ, ἐντύγχανε πρὸς βορέαν τοῖς 𝆴 ὀνόμασι, λέ- γων Ὑπόταξόν μοι πάντα τὰ δαιμόνια, ἵνα μοι ᾖ[2] ὑπήκοος πᾶς δαίμων οὐράνιος καὶ αἰθέριος καὶ ἐπίγειος καὶ ὑπόγειος καὶ χερσαῖος καὶ ἔνυδρος καὶ πᾶσα ἐπιπομπὴ καὶ μάστιξ[3] θεοῦ. Καὶ ἔσται σοι τὰ δαιμόνια πάντα ὑπήκοα. Ἐστὶν δὲ τὸ ἀγαθὸν ζῴδιον.

Goodwin's Translation

An address to the god drawn upon the letter.

I call thee, the headless one, that didst create earth and heaven, that didst create night and day, thee the creator of light and darkness. Thou art Osoronnophris, whom no man hath seen at any time; thou art Iabas, thou art Iapōs, thou hast distinguished the just

and the unjust, thou didst make female and male, thou didst produce seeds and fruits, thou didst make men to love one another and to hate one another. I am Moses thy prophet, to whom thou didst commit thy mysteries, the ceremonies of Israel; thou didst produce the moist and the dry and all manner of food. Listen to me: I am an angel of Phapro Osoronnophris; this is thy true name, handed down to the prophets of Israel. Listen to me, ...
. . . . hear me and drive away this spirit.

I call thee the terrible and invisible god residing in the empty wind, ...
thou headless one, deliver such an one from the spirit that possesses him. . . . .
. . . . strong one, headless one, deliver such an one from the spirit that possesses him . . . .
. . . .
deliver such an one   . . . .
This is the lord of the gods, this is the lord of the world, this is he whom the winds fear, this is he who made voice by his commandment, lord of all things, king, ruler, helper, save this soul
. . . .
. . . . angel of God . . . .
. . . . I am the headless spirit, having sight in my feet, strong, the immortal fire; I am the truth; I am he that hateth that ill-deeds should be done in the world; I am he that lighteneth and thundereth; I am he whose sweat is the shower that falleth upon the earth that it may teem; I am he whose mouth ever burneth; I am the begetter and the bringer forth (?); I am the Grace of the World; my name is the heart girt with a serpent. Come forth and follow. – The celebration of the preceding ceremony. – Write the names upon a piece of new paper, and having extended it over your forehead from one temple to the other, address yourself turning towards the north to the six names, saying: Make all the spirits subject to me, so that every spirit of heaven and of the air, upon the earth and under the earth, on dry land and in the water, and every spell and scourge of God, may be obedient to me. – And all the spirits shall be obedient to you . . . .

Appendix II

A GREEK RITUAL OF MAGIC

Introduction

This essay was written over forty-five years ago. It was published first in *The Occult Review* in London, and recently was republished by Gareth Knight in his excellent periodical *New Dimensions*.

It is included in this book, not because of the simple fact that it is about dramatic rituals, but because in a larger sense *all* rituals are dramatic, at least they should be in order to be effective. This is evidenced, for example, in the Eucharistic ritual on an earlier page, based on fundamental simple formulae that eventuate in a dramatic climax.

The word 'dramatic' as here used implies only that type of ritual or ceremony in which several celebrants are used, as it were, as in the theatre. The ritual elaborated on in this essay, based on Gilbert Murray's superb translation of *The Bacchae* of Euripides, is a good example of this definition. Most of the essay is an extenuation upon that single point.

What is important to emphasize here, however, is that ritual in my common usage of the term is ceremonial magic, and since my experience with the latter is predicated upon fifty years of association with the Hermetic Order of the Golden Dawn and with Aleister Crowley, it includes or utilizes all the methods and techniques of ceremonial such as are described extensively in this book.

At first sight, it may not appear that these methods would be at all necessary in drama. But once it is recognized that all the appurtenances of ceremonial magic are the technical means whereby, on the one hand, considerable power is evoked, and, on the other, the student is exalted to a higher level of consciousness, then it is quite clear that they perform an enormously significant role in ritual, and especially dramatic ritual.

Solely as a preliminary argument, one absolutely essential to clarify all major issues, it is necessary to indicate that, as the text of the essay points out, the Adeptus Minor Ritual of the Golden Dawn is a perfect example of a dramatic ritual. Whatever may or may not be said about S. L. MacGregor Mathers, it was his genius that gave birth to this ritual. It is of course true that the essentials of that dramatic ritual were borrowed from one of the early Rosicrucian classics, as Ellic Howe has pointed out in his most destructive criticism of the Golden Dawn. But I must hasten to add that Mathers was not under any kind of obligation as a magician or as an artist to borrow anything from the *Fama Fraternatitas* other than what would lend itself to his primary intention – to prepare an initiatory ritual in ceremonial and dramatic form. Without the initiated point of view such as Mathers possessed, nothing of this makes any sense. The non-initiate might just as well leave the whole subject alone, for his or her academic and scholastic viewpoint will only make the subject seem ludicrous – but in the long run make him or her a ridiculous laughing stock.

Apart from Ellic Howe's rather ridiculous book on the Golden Dawn, the most recent example of the futility of unilluminated scholarship is demonstrated by Frances A. Yates in her book *The Rosicrucian Enlightenment*. When discussing this recently with a scholarly friend of mine, he remarked 'But the book is so well documented'. Documented indeed! So well documented that it reminded me of a fantastically amusing satire and parody of the well-documented book in one of Aleister Crowley's earliest writings. It is entitled 'The Excluded Middle: or, The Sceptic Refuted' in Volume 1 of his *Collected Works*. It is a dialogue in which almost every word used has a footnote demonstrating not merely the meaning of the word, but giving a pseudo-literary authority for its usage. It is absolutely hilarious. I think Crowley, in the first couple of years of this century, has made an excellent point that is as true to-day as it was then. Scholarship *can* be abused – and *is* often abused.

For instance, Frances Yates, after an enlightening and revealing survey of some sixteenth- and seventeenth-century history relative to the relationship of the Palatinate kings and the kings of England, prior to the appearance of the three Rosicrucian classics, then remarks:

> The story of Christian Rosencreutz and his R.C. Brothers and of the opening of the magic vault containing his tomb was not intended to be taken as literally true by the framer of the manifestoes who were obviously drawing on legends of buried treasure, miraculously rediscovered, such as were particularly prevalent in the alchemical tradition. There is ample evidence in the texts themselves that the story was an allegory or fiction.

Yes — but an allegory of what? Buried treasure as such? Or the rediscovery of the golden treasure in the heart of man which the dramatic ritual — as perceived by the genius of Mathers, and perhaps by some others — was intended to excavate and exalt to the highest.

Yates' prosaic scholarship descends to the totally inane when she remarks 'the opening of the door of the vault symbolizes the opening of a door in Europe'.

The opening of the door of Europe indeed! She recovers sufficiently from her own academic inanity to realize that there *might* be a great deal more — but of this she says but little because, unlike Mathers, she has nothing to say.

Two specific facts of the utmost important must be kept in mind during the following discussion. The first one is that the Vault of the Adepts, so called, is the essential dramatic focus of the Adeptus Minor Ritual. It is described in full in *The Golden Dawn*. Every year, on Corpus Christi day, this Vault was consecrated anew, with the officiating Adept officer assuming the role of the newly initiated Candidate who is bound to the Cross upon which he pledges himself to his higher and divine Genius. The Consecration of this Vault is none other than the basic ritual described in a half a dozen different ways in this book. It is often referred to as 'Opening by Watchtower'. But by whatever name it is called, it is the means whereby the Vault was consecrated, not to represent the opening of Europe to the Reformation and to the newly developing Science of the Middle Ages, but to the service of the Order to the highest divine possibility of its members and of mankind.

It is imperative to stress this as strongly as I can. The Vault, unconsecrated by the invocation of the higher powers of the Elements as described in an earlier chapter here, is merely a vault, a wooden box, with colours painted on it, a piece of theatrical furniture with no virtue in and for itself. Like a talisman, it is merely an object, worthless and dead – regardless of its beauty and aesthetic value. The function of the Consecrating ceremony is to endow what is dead and worthless with life and vitality and spirit, to give it *meaning*.

The Vault ceremony and the entire Adeptus Minor Ritual are dramatic ceremonies which, like all other dramatic rituals – regardless of how beautiful and moving they may be – need to be blessed and consecrated in one form or another until they become *alive*. Several segments of this essay, as the reader will divine, constantly emphasize that the dramatic ritual described is not unrelated (from the 'meaning' viewpoint) to the Adeptus Minor Ritual. As such the drama is in need of the Consecration and Invocations described at length here.

To sum up briefly, the dramatic ritual, like the Vault ceremony, the Adeptus Minor ceremony, or *The Bacchae*, depends for full theurgic efficacy on the use of all such magical and technical methods which comprise the entire content and tenor of this book. Never let this be forgotten. *The Bacchae* is included in this collection of magical reflections for this very reason.

A Greek Ritual of Magic: The Bacchae

To one intent upon the impartial investigations of religions in order to discern the fundamental unity underlying every religious system and philosophy, a study of one of the great tragedies of Euripides presents a number of luminous parallels and noteworthy ideas of tremendous significance. It is a commonplace long familiar almost to everyone that in nearly all religions there is the oft-recurring legend concerning the divine birth of its great founder. Or, perhaps, by way of variation, that at least one of the parents was a high divinity. The virgin birth of Jesus Christ for example, whose mother was visited by the Holy Ghost, appears not so extremely dissimilar, where the essential fact is concerned, to that of Dionysus the thyrsus-bearing hero of *The Bacchae*. The myth, so admirably expressed in Gilbert Murray's *Notes on The Bacchae*, informs us that the mother of Dionysus, Semele, being loved by Zeus the Father of all the gods on the holy mount of Olympus, asked her god-like lover to appear to her in the full glory of his splendour. He came, not as did Gabriel to Mary, nor in the form of a pale dove – but as a glittering white blaze of miraculous lightning. So beyond human endurance was this vision, so exalted was she in the ecstasy of this superhuman experience, that Semele died – not before however giving premature birth to a son.

In the gracious poetical form wherein Euripides has enshrined his immortal tragedy, one finds a presaging of the oriental Avatara theory. Within the person of Dionysus there appears to be not simply one personality, one being, but two very definite and distinct personalities. One is more or less mortal, possessed of human frailties and weaknesses; whereas the other is a divine intelligence of superlative wisdom – a God from the topmost heights of the magical mount. Although the names Bacchus and Dionysus are utilized normally to signify one and the same personage who is the central figure of this poetic creation, and are therefore synonymous, yet I wish arbitrarily to differentiate between them for a brief moment in order to demonstrate the existence of the concept of an Avatara. To Dionysus, let us attribute the character of a man – a wise and highly developed or evolved being, in harmony with current theosophical and magical doctrine, one who, having taken destiny into his own hands aeons and aeons ago, by means of a mystical process of spiritual training and interior development, has consciously opened the gates of his being to a transcendental spiritual self, thus obtaining a relative state of human perfection.

Bacchus, on the other hand, could be termed a God in all actuality. Or, if we wish to use the terminology of Jungian psychology, a primordial archetype of the Collective Unconscious. From the theurgic point of view, that could imply a being who, in periods of evolutionary effort long since ended, and thus representing pages torn out from historical record, obtained complete liberation from the cycle of necessity. Transcending all human ties, he becomes one of the hierarchical psychic forces governing some particular aspect of the universe, the sum total of whose intelligence constitutes what we call Nature.

These two beings, Dionysus the man and Bacchus the God, because of certain persisting spiritual affinities, coalesced for a more or less limited period of time, together forming one consciousness, human and divine and cosmic in its scope and significance. The incarnation two thousand years ago at Nazareth was, according to the philosophy of Rudolf Steiner, just such a conjunction of two individualities who, mingling their essences, became known as Jesus Christ. Shri Krishna of ancient India was another Avatara, as is borne out by the Bhagavad Gita – an incarnation of Vishnu. And the name of Bhagavan Ramakrishna Paramahamsa enjoys also, in some quarters, the reputation of being another and more modern representative of those rare combinations of spirituality and wisdom which incarnate from time to time on this earth for the redemption of mankind.

I believe this hypothesis is amply corroborated by a study of the text itself, which naturally must be the final arbiter of our deductions. In Professor Murray's splendid translation of *The Bacchae* we find, captured by the Theban soldiery, the young and gracious Dionysus confronting boldly and without fear King Pentheus. In this particular statement of the universal myth, Pentheus is comparable in one sense to King Herod of the Jews, and in another sense to Pontius Pilate before whom Jesus was brought to trial. To mocking gibes and taunts of the worst description is the calm Dionysus subjected, as for example when Pentheus throws ridicule on the legendary virgin birth of the God.

'Tis all his word,
This tale of Dionysus; how that same
Babe that was blasted by the lightning flame
With his dead mother, for that mother's lie,
Was re-conceived, born perfect from the thigh
Of Zeus, and now is God! What call ye these?
Dreams? Gibes of the unknown wanderer? Blasphemies
That crave the very gibbet?

The King demands of him the source of his high inspiration – whence came the revelation which has awakened so exuberantly the religious fervour of his people.

> Their intent and use
> Dionysus oped to me, the Child of Zeus.

Spontaneously came this answer. This implies, clearly and indubitably, that although in the text the human being named Dionysus is speaking, yet he refers to another Dionysus, the heavenly child of Zeus who, tentatively, I have denominated Bacchus, the god who inspired the man with light and life and lofty inspiration from above. There would be no real purpose in stating that Dionysus has inspired him, had he not the deliberate intent in mind of differentiating between his own personality and the divine intelligence who dwelt within him.

> Most clear he stood, and scanned
> My soul, and gave his emblems to mine hand.

Thus Dionysus describes the revelation and vision of which he was so recently the recipient. Again, it is quite clear from this that an entity quite apart from his own self is implied. There are two quite distinct entities referred to by Euripides. But Pentheus – the symbol of the conscious ego, of scornful and complacent scepticism, of self-sufficiency and respectability, and representing also the established order of things – consumed with personal pride and violently angry because of the strange rumours rife in his kingdom, remarks that:

> our own
> Wives, our own sisters, from their hearths are flown
> To wild and secret rites; and cluster there
> High on the shadowy hills, with dance and prayer
> To adore this new-made God, this Dionyse...

He is suspicious of this religious revival. Therefore he orders the fair and gentle youth to be enchained. Here we have poetically portrayed the psychological mechanism of repression. The instincts and the vital powers that well up from the primitive unconscious fascinate and yet frighten the ego, the conscious aspect of the psyche. Not understanding the worth and value of the emotional life upon which its own existence rests, and fearful of the dynamic and kinetic quality implicit within the urges which it feels working upon it from without, consciousness instigates a policy of repression and suppression and inhibition. Mocked, reviled, accused of trickery and charlatanism as were all his great predecessors as well as successors, Dionysus is asked whether he actually saw the God and in what form he had appeared.

> What guise
> It liked him. 'Twas not I ordained his shape,

replies Dionysus with subtle confidence, and an underlying contempt for his would-be oppressor. His forehead wreathed with vine tendrils, the broad leaves spreading over his brow, reveals him superficially an effeminate figure, especially with the fawn-skin enveloping his form. As Pentheus first observes:

> Marry, a fair shape for a woman's eye,
> Sir stranger! And thou seek'st no more, I ween!
> Long curls, withal! That shows thou ne'er hast been
> A wrestler! – down on both cheeks so softly tossed
> And winsome! And a white skin! It hath cost
> Thee pains, to please thy damsels with this white
> And red of cheeks that never face the light!

But behind those leaves sharp horns are hidden. And within that delicate and frail-appearing form, despite pale cheeks and curly hair, lurks a mighty spiritual splendour, a fiery will, imperiously demanding absolute obedience. A good picture of the dynamic and intoxicating quality of the Unconscious.

Perchance it would be a transgression were I to repeat the whole theme at length, particularly when it has already been so perfectly described with such sympathy and insight by Walter Pater in his *Greek Studies*. And moreover, there is the unexcelled text which has been translated with such remarkable fluency and rhythm and beauty by Professor Gilbert Murray. Words indeed cannot adequately describe the eloquence which has been brought to bear upon this translation. It is more than literal translation. Within those pages of the English poetic version Murray has caught the whole of the Dionysian spirit – its overflowing vitality, its intoxication and inspiration – with such a virile spontaneity and luxuriance as to be indicative not so much of mere literal translation but of personal artistic creation. However – a literary criticism of this work is not to be essayed here for that momentous task has already been more than adequately accomplished.

The Bacchae as Magical Ritual

There is another aspect, however, of *The Bacchae* which is seldom expounded by its enthusiasts nor by those devotees of Greek drama who delight in the liquid music of its verse. It is the magical aspect to which I make particular reference. In this mystery play it is certain that a significant magical doctrine of paramount importance is concealed, altogether apart from the theoretical details of a spiritual philosophy. Underlying the play and its theatrical performance is an occult presupposition. In short, experience claims and demonstrates of *The Bacchae* that it may be employed satisfactorily as a magical ritual.

From the magical point of view, the basic purpose and object of ritual and invocation is the calling forth of a God, and the conjoining of the human consciousness with the essence of that God. Psychologically, it may be defined as a means of bringing into the bright light of consciousness the repressed concealed side of the psyche. By means of bringing about an assimilation in consciousness of the vast content of the Unconscious, the ego is freed from an infantile attitude towards life and from a compulsive bond of union with nature. It becomes able for the first time to sever the unconscious tie of the *participation mystique*. In a word, it is a method of uniting the ego with its own divine essence and root so that man becomes a fully self-conscious individual.

The Bacchae, then, is a ceremony, the purport of which is the invocation of that primordial archetype of the Unconscious, that spiritual presence which by the Greeks was denominated Zagreus-Dionysus, Sabazios and Bacchus, but which other peoples in different ages and different climes have conceived of and named in other ways. With the Hindus that praeterhuman presence is named Rama and Krishna and Hari. To the ancient dwellers of the Mediterranean and the inhabitants of hither Asia it was known as Tammuz, Attis, Adonis, Osiris and Mithra, and all the other divinities who, in one way or another, concern the so-called solar myth. The theme of the Asiatic or 'dying' God, which Sir James G. Frazer has so admirably expounded in *The Golden Bough*, is in direct relation with the doctrine at issue. Some years ago, Maurice Maeterlinck excellently epitomized this same concept. 'Dionysus... is Osiris, Krishna, Buddha,' he declares, 'He is all the divine incarnations; he is the god who descends into or rather manifests himself in man; and is death, temporary and illusory, and rebirth, actual and immortal; he is the temporary union with the divine that is but the prelude to the final union...' In *The Bacchae* may be discerned a dramatic ceremony of the same order as, for example, the Third Degree of the Masonic Blue Lodge, the Mass of Catholic Christianity, and the Adeptus Minor Ritual of the but rarely heard of Hermetic Order of the Golden Dawn. To wit, the commemoration and invocation of a god, for the resurrection of man's deeper hidden self from the dark tomb of obscurity and mortality.

The Three Aspects of Ritual

One must lay down, first of all, the preliminary hypothesis that the major operations of Theurgy have not even the remotest connection with the production of curious objective phenomena as some erroneously have supposed; nor with dubious feats of psychism or mediumship. Neither has Magic, in this sense, aught to do with what passes today as Spiritualism. The attainment in a mystical rapturous experience of a state of spiritual consciousness is the highest accomplishment of all magical procedure. In the ecstasy of this incomparable experience, known to saints and artists of every age and clime, there is a union of the essence of the microcosm with that greater all-encompassing consciousness which some have variously named God, Spirit, or the Soul of the World.

Now magical ritual possesses three aspects by which this union ensues. The first is a union with a particular deity by means of love, service and devotion. All that which is petty and mean and human is restrained from manifestation; it is a method which may be summarized by the Hindu term *Bhakta*. Here it is necessary to register an emphatic disagreement with Evelyn Underhill. In her work entitled *Mysticism*, Miss Underhill recognizes the fact that will and imagination enter no little into magical work. Yet she is inclined to believe that the Theurgist has but little place for love in his ceremonial operations. This is altogether a false assumption. For how could a god, a being one aspect of whose nature is love itself, be successfully invoked if within the devotee there did not burn a steady flame of the self-same love? In magical ritual worthy of that name, love must occupy an enormous role.

In the second method, a straightforward simple ceremonial is employed, such as that which figures in the *Heptameron* of Peter de Abano, the so-called *Goetia* or *The Lesser Key of King Solomon*, and other textbooks of magical instruction and ritual. By this method, one calls forth from the Astral Light or the Collective Unconscious, with the aid of a trained imaginative faculty and a concentrated will, various of the hierarchies of lesser spiritual beings.

These may legitimately be compared to the constellation of associated ideas or autonomous complexes lurking in the unconscious. With them is locked up a vast store of energy, memory and idea. So long as they are unknown, no evaluation of their worth can be made. Render them accessible to consciousness, however, and, if they can be assimilated, at once you have enriched the psyche, expanded its horizon, and enhanced its nature. By means of their enforced incarnation within the consciousness of the Theurgist, these 'spirits' or archetypes imbue him with the requisite potential of force, thus impelling him in the predetermined direction.

From an analysis of its rituals, there can hardly be imputed a sound metaphysical basis to this method, and its philosophy is extremely crude, to state it mildly. The magician conceives of someone he calls God, upon whom attend a series of angelic beings, variously called archangels, elementals, demons, etc. By simply calling upon this God with a great deal of ado, and commemorating the efforts of previous magicians and saints who accomplished their wonders or attained to the realization of their desires through the invocation of the several names of that God, the magician too realizes the fulfilment of his will. Suggestion obviously must be the decisive factor involved here or, at least, must have a great deal to do with the stirring up of the contents of the Unconscious. It is also the theory that the recital of names, the imaging forth of images and ideas of a certain type, and the projection of the will assisted by the ceremony, has the power of vivifying in the astral light those magical forces of which names and images are symbols. Whatever the real psychological explanation of the way in which this particular technique proceeds, there is little doubt that it works. At least, it works for those who comply with the conditions and have trained themselves in the requisite preliminaries.

The dramatic method is the third and finest aspect, principally for the reason that it combines both the above techniques with the working of a group. Moreover it has the sanction of the highest antiquity. Since it is certainly the method of the poet and in accord with the temperament of all artists, it appears to be the most attractive of all. Its drawback, from one point of view, is that several participants are required, all of whom must sink their personalities in the play and train themselves to work in concert.

On the other hand, there is the equally important fact that a group is enabled to generate a greater supply of energy to provide the basis for a spiritual manifestation than is possible for a single person. In practice, the idea is to arrange a play or a ritualistic ceremony wherein is enacted the entire life-cycle of the God or his terrestrial emissary whose spiritual presence one wishes to invoke. The union or identification with the God is accomplished through suggestion, sympathy and the exaltation of consciousness. For the placing of a keen imagination in harmony with that exemplary life cannot but be a powerful stimulus to the psyche. And what was *once* a fact in nature, the previous ascension of the god into heaven (that is, the occurrence of the mystical experience) may again be repeated on earth. It is not inconceivable that a symbolic or dramatic representation of what was formerly a historical spiritual event in a highly revered personality cannot but assist in a reproduction or a recapitulation of that former union by placing the theurgist in sympathy and magical harmony, through the effect upon his imagination, with the upward trend of the play towards the supreme goal. In fine, the magician *imagines* himself in the ceremony to be the deity who has undergone similar experiences. The rituals serve but to suggest and to render more complete the process of identification, so that sight and hearing and intelligence may serve to that end. In the commemoration, or rehearsal of this history, the magician is uplifted on high, and is whirled into the secret domain of the spirit, there seeing things not lawful to tell to the sons of men.

Loss of Ego-consciousness

While, for the average man, it may be difficult to lose his ego-consciousness in the subject of a play or in a piece of theatrical artistry of any description, for those whose temperament so permits this method is indubitably the most satisfactory.

For instance, in the Adeptus Minor ritual of the Golden Dawn, the initiate watches in the third point of the ritual's progress the resurrection of the Adept hierophant from the hidden Pastos or Tomb of Christian Rosenkreutz in the seven sided Vault. Quite unconsciously, he identifies himself through a prodigious effort of will and imagination with the illuminated consciousness of Rosenkreutz, whose medieval adventures are recounted, or with Christ himself, whose mysteries Rosenkreutz attempted to revive. In any event, even if no conscious effort is made apart from aspiring to the higher, an involuntary current of sympathy is aroused which may be sufficient to accomplish the purpose of the ceremony. For the aesthetic appeal to the imagination is almost irresistible.

And the entire action of the dramatic ritual is such that almost despite itself the soul is exalted to the heights, and during that mystical elevation receives the benediction of enlightenment, inspiration and peace. Not always is consciousness of this ecstasy transmitted. There are occasions when several days, weeks, or months are required for the stimulus given to the unconscious aspect of the psyche to penetrate the wall of reserve that has been erected within the Self and produce an effect upon the conscious ego.

Iamblichus, the divine theurgist of Alexandria, speaks of this kind of ritual in *de Mysteriis* as a 'blessed spectacle'. He states that by its means 'the soul acquires another life, energizes according to another energy, and it is then rightly considered as no longer ranking in the order of men. Frequently, likewise, abandoning her own life she exchanges it for the most blessed energy of the Gods'.

With this brief account of the major principles underlying theurgy, let us consider how they may be applied to *The Bacchae* itself. At the very opening of the ceremonial action of this ritual, the principle of Commemoration is employed to awaken through names and ideas the requisite association tracks in the Unconscious, to evoke the primordial archetypes. Before the sacred tomb of his mother, there stands the young adept Dionysus who recounts, in accordance with the principles laid down above, his own history.

> Behold, God's Son is come unto this land
> of Thebes, even I, Dionysus, whom the brand
> of heaven's hot splendour lit to life, when she
> Who bore me, Cadmus' daughter, Semele
> Died here…
>   There by the castle side
> I see her place, the Tomb of the Lightning's Bride.

In the Greek religion of that day, Dionysus was the God of everlasting youth and immortality. He was the genius presiding over the vine, with its correspondence of spiritual inspiration, and the ritual by which he was worshipped was by a kind of apotheosis of intoxication. He is defined by the text:

> He found the liquid shower
> Hid in the grape. He rests man's spirit dim
> From grieving, when the vine exalteth him.
> He giveth sleep to sink the fretful day
> In cool forgetting.

He typifies not only a spiritual principle, but the course of nature as well – her madness, her prodigality and abundance, her supreme joy and vitality. And above all, the god symbolizes her sublime persistence through the mutations of life and death. He is, in a word, a symbol of the spirit itself, that sum total of psychic energy in all its aspects which comprises the nature of man. The play, too, has indirect reference to the dramatisation of spring, when the solar orb comes back to the earth-folk, laden with warmth and light, ripening the wheat and vine in the fields, and bringing to man after the long cold winter the brightness and glory of the Sun. But the Sun was also, among the mystics of every clime, a symbol of certain high aspects of human and divine consciousness, and it was that consciousness which they desired above all to awaken within their hearts.

To suppress, even if but for a moment or two, the ordinary work-a-day consciousness, with its tedium, its inhibitions, its impediment to the expression of the inner self, this was the object of the Dionysiac cult. To supplement it by the plenitude of the all-permanent stream of spiritual life, to submit to the divine power, and effect in consciousness an identification with the sacred essence of Dionysus – such was the intention of the revels of which we have in *The Bacchae* so vivid a description. No stimulus of sense or emotion or mind was omitted to exite and inspire the soul, that the seeds of the new life might manifest from within the dark concealed depths of the psyche.

The purple darkness of night, bright torches illuminating the solitary groves, intoxicating drinks to quieten the mad motion of the brain, orgiastic dances to convulse the limb, making dumb after physical exhaustion the passions and bodily appetites; noble music and inspiring ritual to exalt the soul on high and to exhilarate the spiritual faculties! 'And though the basis clearly enough is physical, yet,' remarks G. Lowes Dickinson, with reference to these mysteries, 'the whole ritual does undoubtedly express that passion to transcend the limitations of human existence.' These are the physical elements of a properly co-ordinated magical ceremony. They are the mnemonic stages so designed as to form a complex though coherent association track as it were, leading the mind from one thing to another towards a divine end.

The ritual's prologue brings us face to face with the magician who, taking the dramatic role of Dionysus, walks by Circe's stream, narrating as in reverie his life-history in such wise as to cause, for the time being, the theurgist to relive in his creative imagination the life of the God – just as, in the Adeptus Minor ritual of the Golden Dawn, the entire history of the movements of Christian Rosenkreutz is narrated. The candidate for initiation hears first of him being sequestered in a monastery, then of his journey eastwards to Damascus, his experiences there, and finally of his return home to Germany with the idea germinating in his mind to formulate an order teaching the knowledge and wisdom he has acquired.

In *The Bacchae* the Chorus of maidens who appear following the departure of Dionysus, fills in the picture to complete for the actors or participants in the rite the details as to whom the god is, and for what spiritual principles he stands. They sing:

> Hither, O fragrant of Tmolus the Golden,
>   Come with the voice of timbrel and drum;
> Let the cry of your joyance uplift and embolden
>   The God of the joy-cry; O Bacchanals, come!
> With pealing of pipes and with Phrygian clamour,
>   On, where the vision of holiness thrills,
> And the music climbs and the maddening glamour,
>   With the wild white maids, to the hills, to the hills!
> Oh, then, like a colt as he runs by a river,
>   A colt by his dam, when the heart of him sings,
> With the keen limbs drawn and the fleet foot a-quiver,
>   Away the Bacchanal springs!

Those celebrants enacting the parts of the intoxicated Maenads – if they have performed aright the imaginative work of formulating vivid images which act as a magnet to the libido stored within the archetypal images in the unconscious, and if they are able to lose themselves completely in the dance, subordinating their own personal ego to the suggestion of the play – should likewise experience some faint adumbration of that exuberance and ecstatic frenzy which this song peals for us. For frenzy was a state specially to be cultivated, as being the means whereby the ego submerged itself in a larger fuller life. 'Prophecy cleaves to all frenzy, but beyond all else to frenzy of prayer. Then in us verily dwells the God himself, and speaks the thing to be.' Those who have seen at any time the famous Isadora Duncan, or Anna Pavlova dance her ballet divertissement 'The Bacchanale' will have some fair idea of the orgiastic feelings which this sort of dance can engender.

One of the most noteworthy stage directions indicating the real magical nature of the play, is found where the seer Tieresias is in conversation with the aged father of Semele, Cadmus. As the first movements of the Bacchic worship commence, he becomes enamoured with its frenzy, excited as though moved by some extraneous agency. 'A mysterious strength and exaltation enter into him.'

Then follows the grand scene of the drama, which is also the climax of the ritual. The gentle exquisite youth, the human Dionysus with his following composed chiefly of Maenads – temporarily deserted by his guiding genius, the divine Bacchus – seems to threaten, at least in the eyes of enthroned authority, the established order of things. That authority, therefore, takes urgent steps, as always it has striven, to put an end to the upstart. Just as, in the instance of Christ, whose opponents claimed that he set himself up against the Roman Empire, Jesus was brought to trial before Pilate to be mocked and scourged and crowned with a wreath of thorns, so likewise was Dionysus. We find him bound and manacled and thrust into a dark dungeon cell, although Pentheus, the inquisitor, is duly warned of the folly of his tyrranical act by his own father and by the seer Tieresias, in which warning occurs the following philosophic strain:

> List and understand,
> King Pentheus! Dream not thou that force is power;
> Nor, if thou hast a thought, and that thought sour
> And sick, oh, dream not thought is wisdom!

Likewise there is the impassioned appeal by a messenger to do no harm to the young god.

> Oh, let him live;
> For if he die, then Love herself is slain,
> And nothing joyous in the world again!

It would be no difficult matter to recast the form of this play to transform it into a magical ceremony, retaining only those sections or verses which actually touch upon the central theme of the dramatic invocation of the God. Several parts or points would need to be devised. Probably one of the most important would need to be that of traditional Magic. All foreign influences would require to be banished from the Temple or scene of the play by means of the proper conjurations, circumambulations and tracings of lineal figures, such as the pentagram and hexagram. This should be followed by a consecration both of the sphere of operation generally, as well as of every person and object within that purified sphere. Incense and holy oils are of supreme importance in this connection. Then, all these preliminary details completed, would follow the act of invoking the forces pertaining generally to the nature of Dionysus, that of the sphere of the Sun, employing a special invocation to be uttered together with the appropriate invoking hexagram ritual. This would complete the first point of the ceremony. The succeeding portions of the play could be a condensed version of this text, retaining the essential features in the most highly dramatic form imaginable.

After the imprisonment of the god, the scene changes to the secrecy of the thickly-wooded groves, where ensues the mysterious worship of Dionysus. To our unaccustomed gaze, Euripides displays a chorus of dancing Bacchantes invoking eagerly and impatiently, with irresistible frenzy and enthusiasm, their beloved deity to visible appearance.

> Lo, we race with death, we perish
>   Dionysus, here before thee!
> Dost thou mark us not, nor cherish,
>   Who implore thee, and adore thee?
>   Hither down Olympus' side,
>   Come, O Holy One defied,
> Be thy golden wand uplifted o'er the tyrant in his pride.

Amid earthquakes and thunders – probably the theatrical means of giving actual expression to the sequence of sounds heard psychically as the mystical experience occurs – to the accompaniment of invisible voices issuing from the Castle to announce his appearance, the youthful divinity, now enshrined by his genius, appears and upbraids his maenads for their so little faith in him and his power to escape from tyranical imprisonment.

> O cast ye, cast ye, to the earth! The Lord
>   Cometh against this house! Oh, cast ye down,
> Ye trembling damsels; He, our own adored,
> God's child hath come, and all is overthrown!

To his 'damsels of the Morning Hills', to quote the marvellous description of the Bacchantes, he narrates how, when manacled and bound with chains in the castle dungeons – his guardian genius returned. 'A Voice, and lo, our Lord was come,' says Dionysus. Again, it is necessary to recall the reader's attention to the manner in which Dionysus refers to the 'other' who bears his name also. Without a doubt, the play teaches of two distinct beings acting through one personality.

In dire confusion the shackles fell apart, and the Adept infilled by the presence of his divine lord makes good his release from the prison. Faced by the furious and bewildered Pentheus who utters 'I scorn him and his vines,' Dionysus, now inspired, remarks gently: 'For Dionyse 'tis well; for in thy scorn his glory lies.'

He warns the king that in the instigation of repression and persecution he has gone but a step too far, with sage advice suggesting:

> Better to yield him prayer and sacrifice
> Than kick against the pricks since Dionyse
> Is God, and thou but mortal.

Just at this juncture, a king's messenger returns to the castle with almost incredible reports of the bands of the dancing Maenads, of their revels and worship, even of miracles that occurred spontaneously without previous deliberation. He told of strange incidents of girls playing with long quick snakes that hissed and writhed with quivering tongues, of others feeding fawns and young wolf cubs with milk from their own maiden breasts.

    And one would raise
Her wand and smite the rock, and straight a jet
Of quick bright water came. Another set
Her thyrsus in the bosomed earth, and there
Was red wine that the God sent up to her,
A darkling fountain. And if any lips
Sought whiter draughts, with dipping finger-tips
They pressed the sod, and gushing from the ground
Came springs of milk, And reed-wands ivy-crowned
Ran with sweet honey, drop by drop.

So it comes about, since the messenger says that if the King had witnessed so holy a scene he would straightaway have gone and worshipped the god, that we approach the secondary crisis of the ritual. The God intimates that perchance Pentheus might wish to see for himself the Dionysian revels celebrated by the Maenads in the fastnesses of the forest groves, and the king, already under the hypnotic spell of the God, acquiesces. That decision is his undoing. Little does he realize that, so intense and unyielding has been his repression, to witness these orgiastic rites can only mean his complete destruction at the hands of an outraged eros. Much to his annoyance, they clothe Pentheus like a Maenad in 'a rich and trailing robe of fine linen', 'a long tress dangling low beneath thy shoulders', the dappled fawn-skin and the ivy thyrsus. Then, with Dionysus accompanying him, he sets out amid secrecy to observe the intoxicating power of the Bacchic revelry.

There is a distinctive psychology of clothing. It is for this reason that magicians everywhere and at all times have employed rich gowns of silk and gorgeously coloured robes. By sympathy, colours and congruous objects may awaken and attract the desired magical forces. It is this important consideration which led certain generations of not highly initiated theurgists to adopt for ceremonial use actual masks, grotesques, and legitimate theatrical artifice. I say not highly initiated advisedly, for it is in the imagination and the imagined inner psychic world where belong these formulated shapes and colours of gods and angelic beings. But coloured gowns have an efficacy quite apart from their imagined effect – as demonstrated, in a somewhat similar way, by the use of different coloured rays and lights in therapeutic work.

And while it may be that Euripides causes Pentheus to assume the garb of Maenad solely as disguise in order that his presence may not be divined by the fanatical adherents of the Dionysiac cult, there is nevertheless the significant fact concerning clothing here mentioned which is not often realized. The dappled fawn-skin may quite reasonably represent the chasuble or mantle worn over the fine linen gown which is the magical robe; the tresses and the snood constitute in one sense the nemyss or head-dress, and the ivy thyrsus is his wand. In theurgy, the wand is the symbol of the will – in this case, a sensuous and inhibited animal will, dangerous and prone to explosive moods. Clad like a Bacchante, Pentheus becomes singularly excited, the spirit of the Dionysian frenzy slowly overcoming his otherwise rational behaviour, like some obsessing compulsive emotion welling up from the deeps. He wildly cries:

> What strength is this!
> Kithaeron's steeps and all that in them is –
> How say'st thou? – Could my shoulders lift the whole?

And now, too, he obtains a fleeting vision of what Dionysus really is. For whereas the god previously seemed to him a weak and effeminate figure he begins to divine a presence which so far from being feeble and girlish and weak is at once divine and strong and terrible.

> Yea; and mine eye
> Is bright! …
> And is it a Wild Bull this, that walks and waits
> Before me? There are horns upon thy brow!
> What art thou, man or beast? For surely now
> The Bull is on thee!

There are parallels to this sort of vision in the clinical experience of modern psychological work. To a child, it may seem that the feelings and emotions are girlish and effeminate principles of his psyche, not to be encouraged because of fear of ridicule and hurt. Consequently a programme of repression is instigated. No longer are the emotions encouraged and expressed. They are stifled and stilled, until eventually, their evocation in adult life is difficult and tedious. But the psychic life of the individual as expressed in the spontaneous activities of his dream life show the enormous power which these repressed contents of the emotional life really possess. Very often, they produce nightmares and horrible gruesome dreams, in which wild animals — bulls, elephants and tigers, representing the cruelly inhibited feelings, play a very active part.

Once again, the point of the ritual closes, and Euripides shifts the scene of the tragedy. The practising theurgists are replunged headlong into the dance of the Maenads who chant their magical invocations. I quote two verses in particular, since these few lines correspond, more so perhaps than any others in the entire play, with the lyrical style which immemorially has been that wherein theurgic conjurations have been couched. The first occurs quite early in the ritual, the second comes much later on.

Up, O Bacchae, wife and maiden,
    Come, O ye Bacchae, come;
O bring the joy bestower,
God-seed of God the Sower,
Bring Bromios in his power
    From Phrygia's mountain dome;
To street and town and tower,
    Oh, bring ye Bromios home!

Appear, appear, whatso thy shape or name
    O Mountain Bull, Snake of the Hundred Heads, Lion of
    Burning Flame!
O God, Beast, Mystery, come! Thy mystic maids
Are hunted! — Blast their hunter with thy breath,
    Cast over his head thy snare;
And laugh aloud and drag him to his death,
Who stalks thy herded madness in its lair!

Again Euripides has recourse to a technicality of stagecraft whereby to convey the death of King Pentheus, thus rendering the dramatic efforts of the magical participants less arduous. A messenger, pale and distraught, enters hastily from the mountains. Bearing the news to the leader of the Chorus, he tells how Pentheus had gone to Kithaeron's slopes with Dionysus to watch while in ambush the mode of Dionysian worship. There the king had been captured by the Maenads, enraged at one spying upon their secret worship. Spurred on by Agave, his own mother – who, however, enraptured by the Bacchic ecstasy knew not what she did, nor did she recognize the royal person of their victim – Pentheus was torn limb from limb by the Bacchantes. As the climax after the tragedy of the death of the principal enemy of the God, there follows then the ascension of Dionysus to heaven upon a cloud – symbolic of spiritual triumph and illumination.

The Solar Significance of The Bacchae

Thus *The Bacchae* ends – upon a lyrical note of magical exaltation. It is an epic, theurgic, religious and philosophic in implication, depicting the triumph and victory of the God over his oppressors. It is therefore a divine history most suitable for ceremonial presentation.

The whole drama is solar in significance. Yet not only astonomically so, but spiritually. In every system of religious philosophy, the Sun represents the symbol of all that is highest, finest, and best in man. Not only is the Sun our father and redeemer even from a physical point of view, but the whole of our inner spiritual existence, which is the real life of us, is intimately bound up in all sorts of ways with that of the sun. As we see it, the Sun is the outer vehicle of the inner spiritual sun; the flaming garment of a God or a hierarchy of gods, of whose nature we are part and parcel. They dwell in us, and we in them, and from their supernal existence we may not be separated even for one instant of time.

The student of ancient religions will have noted the indubitable fact that the great teachers of Magic almost without exception identified with the cycle of the Sun's eternal journey through the heavens. Or rather, to be somewhat more accurate, the cycle of their individual lives attached itself to the greater cycle of the sun. The Nativity at the Winter Solstice and the Crucifixion at the Vernal Equinox are quite obvious in suggesting the birth of the

Saviour and his elevation above the order of physical nature. The Autumnal Equinox, just prior to the going down of the sun to its hiding for the long dark winter, may also suggest to a keen imagination, as it did to the worshippers of Mithra and Dionysus, the obscuration of the Sun and the imprisonment of the God in a dungeon. There are numerous variations upon this one central theme, but the symbols are nearly always equivalent.

Yet since the Sun does simultaneously represent a spiritual value, the theurgists of all time have endeavoured to utilize the recurrence of this divine force for the illumination and advancement of mankind. The methods varied, depending entirely upon the temperament of the people to whom they were endeavouring to pass on their message, and the intelligence of the immediate individuals with whom personally they had magical commerce. In *The Bacchae* of Euripides we may perceive another attempt, and a very fine one indeed, to drive home to the Greeks through the medium of the theatre and by way of tragedy, the same old lesson, the identical teaching which was given to all antiquity.

Symbolism in The Bacchae

The symbolism is far from difficult to trace. Psychologically, it is very descriptive indeed. One may almost detect the entire mechanisms of the Freudian scheme there – from repression and resistance right up, or down, to the Oedipus complex. Pentheus in the ritual is the dramatic representation of ordinary consciousness – that personal egoic faculty which wilfully blinds itself to the limitations of its own power, and to the existence of other powers even within its own household. Since it falsely believes as a matter of habit that it and it alone is the supreme power, and that all else matters not at all, this source of power must be deliberately sacrificed on the mystic altar before illumination can take place. This personal ego endeavours ruthlessly to repress both the divine spirit which is its lord and creator, as well as the natural instincts, of which latter the Maenads, wild, hysterical, and mad that they were, furnish a most apt symbol. If the instincts are too violently repressed, then because of the clogging of the personal unconscious, and because of the explosive tendency which that unconscious develops, consciousness becomes narrow and delimited, and quite unable to receive inspiration and energy from the Collective Unconscious. In the Jungian analysis, it becomes necessary first to analyse away, so to speak, the repressed instincts that have been thrust out of sight. By rendering them accessible to consciousness, it then becomes possible to deal adequately with the Collective Unconscious which was quite distant from treatment before.

This rational consciousness of man, represented in the drama by King Pentheus, in overstepping the legitimate confines of its power and proper activity, is torn into mere shreds of bleeding flesh by those archaic forces he seeks erroneously to repress and thrust out from his kingdom – where, and only where, they truly belong. His own mother, typifying here the inchoate destructive aspect of Nature, being the first to claw at his throat. Psycho-analysis is wealthy with lurid details and innumerable cases of those misguided individuals whose integrity of consciousness has been torn asunder by the repressed unconscious forces of their being. And it almost seems as if Euripides presages – or else had a deep intuitive insight into – the Freudian concept of the passionate mother effect which first of all brings into existence the repression mechanism. It is this repressed mother fixation, around which all subsequent repressed material and emotion constellates by association, that in the long run proves to be the undoing of the unenlightened individual by ruining all his attempts towards social adaptation and the leading of a normally useful life. How profoundly has not Euripides depicted the revenge of the terrible Mother!

Both the King and the Maenads – both ego-consciousness and the instinctual urges – have their rightful place in the scheme of things, each has its respective place in the universe. For the one to usurp or interfere with the true functions of the other is at once to invite chaos and complete disorganization.

Bacchus-Dionysus represents the vital stream of spiritual energy, the totality of man's forces. He represents the Sun in its dual aspect, particularly the symbol of the central intoxicating and ecstatic spirit to be invoked into human consciousness during the ineffable rites. To his services must the Maenads be dedicated. For he is the life of the instincts, that which motivates and directs their movement. Nor should Pentheus interfere with the divinity's true progress, for he can have no notion of the true import and significance of the intentions, teleological and immediate, of the god. Let him not interfere, so that the abounding vitality and never-to-be-exhausted intoxication of the God may freely be shed upon all and sundry.

His ceremonial imprisonment and manacling may refer to two phenomena. One, the loss of spirit, with the consequent neurasthenia, experienced by the neurotic when repression has proceeded too far. And on a higher level of interpretation, to the obscuration of the spiritual self during the 'dark night of the soul'. Only the return of the sun, or the magical descent of the God into the mind, can lift that black night of horror and despair. The self-devised release from prison, with the subsequent death of the tyrant oppressor, likewise has at least two planes of interpretation.

It can quite easily refer to the effect of schizophrenia – the complete splitting of consciousness, and the loss of integrity and sanity – the destruction of King Pentheus. Moreover, in a far deeper sense, it represents the successful appearance of the invoked force and its incarnation within the inmost hearts of its devotees, banishing forever enslavement to the world's complacent and hypocritical attitude towards life and living. On the physical plane, the oncoming of Spring in all its glory for the fructification of all life is seen here, the eternal sanctification and spiritual consecration of every being to that inspiring miracle which year after year proceeds without diminishment and without abatement.

The rehearsal of this tragic history of Euripides' *The Bacchae* implies to the company of theurgists all these doctrines, and exalts the human consciousness beyond its normal bounds and confines. At the same time, by means of the magical invocations, the power of sound applied to the vibration of the Names, and the actual assumption of the astral God-form, the God himself may be called forth, and with his divine essence the company conjoin themselves in bliss.

And the result of this Magic is an acceleration of the development of the Spirit. Whereas long countless ages are required for the evolution and growth of the mass of mankind towards a distant ideal of spiritual perfection, the Magician seeks to further his progress, and to evolve more rapidly to that goal which ultimately must be reached by all. 'The outcome of the telestic union with the Gods is an improvement of every faculty and power of mind in the constitution of man. For the Gods, or the universal essences of light to theurgists in unenvying abundance, call upwards their souls to themselves, procuring them a union with themselves, and accustoming them, while they are yet in a body, to be separated from bodies, and to be led round to their eternal and intelligible principle.'

Appendix III

PRELIMINARY INVOCATION FROM *THE GOETIA*

PRELIMINARY INVOCATION.

Thee I invoke, the Bornless one.
Thee, that didst create the Earth and the Heavens:
Thee, that didst create the Night and the Day.
Thee, that didst create the darkness and the Light.
Thou art Osorronophris: Whom no man hath seen at any time.
Thou art Iâbas
Thou art Iâpôs:
Thou hast distinguished between the just and the Unjust.
Thou didst make the female and the Male.
Thou didst produce the Seed and the Fruit.
Thou didst form Men to love one another, and to hate one another.

I am Mosheh Thy Prophet, unto Whom Thou didst commit
Thy Mysteries, the Ceremonies of Ishrael:
Thou didst produce the moist and the dry, and that which
nourisheth all created Life.
Hear Thou Me, for I am the Angel of Paphrô Osorronophris:
this is Thy True Name, handed down to the Prophets of Ishrael.

N

Hear Me:—
Ar: Thiao: Rheibet: Athelebersheth:
A: Blatha: Abeu: Ebeu: Phi:
Chitasoe: Ib: Thiao.

hear Me, and make all Spirits subject unto Me: so that every Spirit of the Firmament and of the Ether; upon the Earth and under the Earth: on dry Land and in the Water: of Whirling Air, and of rushing Fire: and every Spell and Scourge of God may be obedient unto Me.

ש

I invoke Thee, the Terrible and Invisible God: Who dwellest in the Void Place of the Spirit:—

Arogogorobraō: Sothou:
Modorio: Phalarthaō: Dōō: Ape, The Bornless One:
hear Me: etc.

ר

hear me:—
Roubriaō: Mariōdam: Balbnabaoth: Assalonai: Aphniaō: I:
Tholeth: Abrasar: Aēōōū: Ischure, Mighty and Bornless One!
hear me: etc.

ה

I invoke Thee:—
    Ma: Barraiō: Jōēl: Kotha:
    Athorēbalō: Abraoth:
hear Me: etc.

יון

hear me!
Aōth: Abaōth: Basum: Isak:
Sabaoth: Iao:

This is the Lord of the Gods:
This is the Lord of the Universe:
This is He Whom the Winds fear.

This is he, Who having made Voice by his Commandment, is Lord of All Things; King, Ruler and Helper.

Hear Me, etc.

Hear Me:—

Ieou: Pûr: Iou: Pûr: Iaôt: Iaeô: Ioou: Abrasar: Sabriam: Do: Uu: Adonaie: Ede: Edu: Angelos ton Theon: Anlala Lai: Gaia: Ape: Diathanna Thorun.

I Am He! the Bornless Spirit! having sight in the Feet: Strong, and the Immortal Fire!

I Am He! the Truth!

I Am He! Who hate that evil should be wrought in the World!

I am He, that lighteneth and thundereth.

I am He, from whom is the Shower of the Life of Earth:

I am He, whose mouth ever flameth:

I am He, the Begetter and Manifester unto the Light:

I am He; the Grace of the World:

"The Heart Girt with a Serpent" is My Name!

Come Thou forth, and follow Me: and make all Spirits subject unto Me so that every Spirit of the Firmament, and of the Ether: upon the Earth and under the Earth: on dry land, or in the Water: of whirling Air or of rushing Fire: and every Spell and Scourge of God, may be obedient unto me!

Iao: Sabao:

Such are the Words!

Appendix IV

LIBER SAMEKH BY ALEISTER CROWLEY

LIBER SAMEKH

Theurgia Goetia Summa

(CONGRESSUS CUM DAEMONE)

sub figura DCCC

being the Ritual employed by the Beast 666 for the Attainment of the Knowledge and Conversation of his Holy Guardian Angel during the Semester of His performance of the Operation of the Sacred Magick of ABRAMELIN THE MAGE.

(Prepared An XVII ☉ in ♍ at the Abbey of Thelema in Cephalaedium by the Beast 666 in service to FRATER PROGRA-DIOR.)

OFFICIAL PUBLICATION OF A∴ A∴ Class D for the Grade of Adeptus Minor.

POINT

I

EVANGELII TEXTUS REDACTUS

The Invocation.

Magically restored, with the significance of the

BARBAROUS NAMES

Etymologically or Qabalistically determined and paraphrased in English.

Section A. **The Oath.**

1. Thee I invoke, the Bornless One.
2. Thee, that didst create the Earth and the Heavens.
3. Thee, that didst create the Night and the Day.
4. Thee, that didst create the darkness and the Light.
5. Thou art ASAR UN-NEFER ('Myself made Perfect'):
   Whom no man hath seen at any time.
6. Thou art IA-BESZ ('the Truth in Matter').
7. Thou art IA-APOPHRASZ ('the Truth in Motion').
8. Thou hast distinguished between the Just and the Unjust.
9. Thou didst make the Female and the Male.
10. Thou didst produce the Seeds and the Fruit.
11. Thou didst form Men to love one another, and to hate one another.

Section Aa.

1. I am ANKH - F - N - KHONSU thy Prophet, unto Whom Thou didst commit Thy Mysteries, the Ceremonies of KHEM.
2. Thou didst produce the moist and the dry, and that which nourisheth all created Life.
3. Hear Thou Me, for I am the Angel of PTAH-APOPHRASZ-RA (vide the Rubric): this is Thy True Name, handed down to the Prophets of KHEM.

Section B.   **Air.**

Hear Me: —

AR	'O breathing, flowing Sun!'
ThIAF[1]	'O Sun IAF! O Lion-Serpent Sun, The Beast that whirlest forth, a thunderbolt, begetter of Life!'
RhEIBET	'Thou that flowest! Thou that goest!'
A-ThELE-BER-SET	'Thou Satan-Sun Hadith that goest without Will!'
A	'Thou Air! Breath! Spirit! Thou without bound or bond!'
BELAThA	'Thou Essence, Air Swift-streaming, Elasticity!'
ABEU	'Thou Wanderer, Father of All!'
EBEU	'Thou Wanderer, Spirit of All!'
PhI-ThETA-SOE	'Thou Shining Force of Breath! Thou Lion-Serpent Sun! Thou Saviour, save!'
IB	'Thou Ibis, secret solitary Bird, inviolate Wisdom, whose Word is Truth, creating the World by its Magick!'
ThIAF	'O Sun IAF! O Lion-Serpent Sun, The Beast that whirlest forth, a thunderbolt, begetter of Life!'

(The conception is of Air, glowing, inhabited by a Solar-Phallic Bird, 'the Holy Ghost', of a Mercurial Nature.)

Hear me, and make all Spirits subject unto Me; so that every Spirit of the Firmament and of the Ether: upon the Earth and under the Earth, on dry land and in the water; of Whirling Air, and of rushing Fire, and every Spell and Scourge of God may be obedient unto Me.

---

1. The letter F is used to represent the Hebrew Vau and the Greek Digamma; its sound lies between those of the English long o and long oo, as in Rope and Tooth.

Section C.   **Fire.**

I invoke Thee, the Terrible and Invisible God: Who dwellest in the
Void Place of the Spirit: —

AR-O-GO-GO-RU-ABRAO	'Thou spiritual Sun! Satan, Thou Eye, Thou Lust! Cry aloud! Cry aloud! Whirl the Wheel, O my Father, O Satan, O Sun!'
SOTOU	'Thou, the Saviour!'
MUDORIO	'Silence! Give me Thy Secret!'
PhALARThAO	'Give me suck, Thou Phallus, Thou Sun!'
OOO	'Satan, thou Eye, thou Lust!' 'Satan, thou Eye, thou Lust!' 'Satan, thou Eye, thou Lust!'
AEPE	'Thou self-caused, self-determined, exalted, Most High!'

The Bornless One.   (Vide supra).
(The conception is of Fire, glowing, inhabited by a Solar-Phallic
Lion of a Uranian nature.)
Hear Me, and make all Spirits subject unto Me: so that every Spirit
of the Firmament and of the Ether: upon the Earth and under the
Earth: on dry Land and in the Water: of whirling Air, and of
rushing Fire, and every Spell and Scourge of God may be obedient
unto Me.

Section D.   **Water.**

Hear Me: —

RU-ABRA-IAF[1]	'Thou the Wheel, thou the Womb, that containeth the Father IAF!'
MRIODOM	'Thou the Sea, the Abode!'
BABALON-BAL-BIN-ABAFT.	'Babalon! Thou Woman of Whoredom!' 'Thou, Gate of the Great God ON! Thou Lady of the Understanding of the Ways!'

1. See, for the formula of IAF, or rather FIAOF, Book 4 Part III, Chapter V.
The form FIAOF will be found preferable in practice.

ASAL-ON-AI	'Hail Thou, the unstirred! Hail, sister and bride of ON, of the God that is all and is none, by the Power of Eleven!'
APhEN-IAF	'Thou Treasure of IAO!'
I	'Thou Virgin twin-sexed! Thou Secret Seed! Thou inviolate Wisdom!'
PhOTETh	'Abode of the Light . . . .
ABRASAX	' ... of the Father, the Sun, of Hadith, of the spell of the Aeon of Horus!'
AEOOU	'Our Lady of the Western Gate of Heaven!'
ISChURE	'Mighty art Thou!'

Mighty and Bornless One!   (Vide Supra)

(The conception is of Water, glowing, inhabited by a Solar-Phallic Dragon-Serpent, of a Neptunian nature.)

Hear Me: and make all Spirits subject unto Me: so that every Spirit of the Firmament and of the Ether: upon the Earth and under the Earth: on dry Land and in the Water: of whirling Air, and of rushing Fire: and every Spell and Scourge of God may be obedient unto Me.

Section E.   **Earth.**

I invoke Thee: —

MA	'O Mother! O Truth!'
BARRAIO	'Thou Mass!'[1]
IOEL	'Hail, Thou that art!'
KOThA	'Thou hollow one!'
AThOR-e-BAL-O	'Thou Goddess of Beauty and Love, whom Satan, beholding, desireth!'

1. 'Mass', in the sense of the word which is used by physicists. The impossibility of defining it will not deter the intrepid initiate (in view of the fact that the fundamental conception is beyond the normal categories of reason.)

ABRAFT   'The Fathers, male-female, desire Thee!'
(The conception is of Earth, glowing, inhabited by a Solar-Phallic
Hippopotamus[1] of a Venereal nature.)
Hear Me: and make all Spirits subject unto Me: so that every Spirit
of the Firmament, and of the Ether: upon The Earth and under the
Earth: on dry land and in the Water: of Whirling Air, and of
rushing Fire: and every Spell and Scourge of God may be obedient
unto Me.

Section F.   **Spirit.**

Hear Me:

AFT   'Male-Female Spirits!'

ABAFT   'Male-Female Sires!'

BAS-AUMGN.   'Ye that are Gods, going forth, uttering
                              AUMGN. (The Word that goeth from
                              (A) Free Breath.
                              (U) through Willed Breath.
                              (M) and Stopped Breath.
                              (GN) to Continuous Breath.
                              thus symbolizing the whole course of
                              spiritual life. A is the formless Hero; U is
                              the six-fold solar sound of physical life,
                              the triangle of Soul being entwined with
                              that of Body; M is the silence of 'death';
                              GN is the nasal sound of generation &
                              knowledge.)

ISAK   'Identical Point!'

SA-BA-FT   'Nuith! Hadith! Ra-Hoor-Khuit!'
                              'Hail, Great Wild Beast!'
                              'Hail, IAO!'

1. Sacred to AHAThOOR. The idea is that of the Female conceived as
invulnerable, reposeful, of enormous swallowing capacity etc.

Section Ff.

1. This is the Lord of the Gods:
2. This is the Lord of the Universe:
3. This is He whom the Winds fear.
4. This is He, Who having made Voice by His commandment is Lord of all Things; King, Ruler and Helper. Hear Me, and make all Spirits subject unto Me: so that every Spirit of the Firmament and of the Ether: upon the Earth and under the Earth: on dry Land and in the Water: of whirling Air, and of rushing Fire: and every Spell and Scourge of God may be obedient unto Me.

Section G.   **Spirit.**

Hear Me: —

IEOU	'Indwelling Sun of Myself'
PUR	'Thou Fire! Thou Sixfold Star initiator compassed about with Force and Fire!'
IOU	'Indwelling Soul of Myself'
PUR	(Vide Supra)
IAFTh	'Sun-lion Serpent, hail! All Hail, thou Great Wild Beast, thou IAO!'
IAEO	'Breaths of my Soul, breaths of mine Angel.'
IOOU	'Lust of my Soul, lust of mine Angel!'
ABRASAX	(Vide Supra).
SABRIAM	'Ho for the Sangraal! Ho for the Cup of Babalon! Ho for mine Angel pouring Himself forth within my Soul!'
OO	'The Eye! Satan, my Lord! The Lust of the Goat!'
FF	'Mine Angel! Mine initiator! Thou one with me – the Sixfold Star!'
AD-ON-A-I[1]	'My Lord! My secret self beyond self, Hadith, All Father! Hail, ON, thou Sun, thou Life of Man, thou Fivefold Sword

1. In Hebrew, ADNI, 65. The Gnostic Initiates transliterated it to imply their own secret formulae; we follow so excellent an example. ON is an Arcanum of

of Flame! Thou Goat exalted upon Earth
in Lust, thou Snake extended upon Earth
in Life! Spirit most holy! Seed most
Wise! Innocent Babe. Inviolate Maid!
Begetter of Being! Soul of all Souls!
Word of all Words, Come forth, most
hidden Light!'

EDE   'Devour thou me!'

EDU   'Thou dost devour Me!'

ANGELOS TON ThEON   'Thou Angel of the Gods!'

ANLALA   'Arise thou in Me, free flowing, Thou
                       who art Naught, who art Naught, and
                       utter thy Word!'

LAI   'I also am Naught! I Will Thee! I behold
                       Thee! My nothingness!'

GAIA   'Leap up, thou Earth!'
                       (This is also an agonising appeal to the
                       Earth, the Mother; for at this point of the
                       ceremony the Adept should be torn from
                       his mortal attachments, and die to himself
                       in the orgasm of his operation.[1])

AEPE   'Thou Exalted One! It (i.e. the spiritual
                       'semen', the Adept's secret ideas, drawn
                       irrisistably from their 'Hell'[2] by the love
                       of his Angel) leaps up; it leaps forth![3]

Arcana; its significance is taught, gradually, in the O.T.O. Also AD is the paternal
formula, Hadit; ON is its complement NUIT; the final Yod signifies 'mine'
etymologically and essentially the Mercurial (transmitted) hermaphroditic virginal
seed – The Hermit of the Taro – The use of the name is to invoke one's own inmost
secrecy, considered as the result of the conjunction of Nuit and Hadit. If the second A
is included, its import is to affirm the operation of the Holy Ghost and the
formulation of the Babe in the Egg, which precedes the appearance of the Hermit.

   1.   A thorough comprehension of Psycho-analysis will contribute notably to the
proper appreciation of this Ritual.

   2.   It is said among men that the word Hell deriveth from the word 'helan', to
hele or conceal, in the tongue of the Anglo-Saxons. That is, it is the concealed
place, which since all things are in thine own self, is the unconscious. Liber CXI
(Aleph) cap Δ ς.

   3.   But compare the use of the same word in section C.

DIATHARNA   'Lo! the out-splashing of the seeds of
THORON   Immortality!'

Section Gg.   The Attainment.

1. I am He! the Bornless Spirit! having sight in the feet: Strong, and the Immortal Fire!
2. I am He! the Truth!
3. I am He! Who hate that evil should be wrought in the World!
4. I am He, that lighteneth and thundereth!
5. I am He, from whom is the Shower of the Life of Earth!
6. I am He, whose mouth ever flameth!
7. I am He, the Begetter and Manifester unto the Light!
8. I am He, The Grace of the Worlds!
9. 'The Heart Girt with a Serpent' is my name!

Section H   The 'Charge to the Spirit'.

Come thou forth, and follow me: and make all Spirits subject unto Me so that every Spirit of the Firmament, and of the Ether, upon the Earth and under the Earth: on dry Land, or in the Water: of whirling Air or of rushing Fire, and every Spell and Scourge of God, may be obedient unto me!

Section J.   The Proclamation of the Beast 666.

IAF: SABAF[1]
     Such are the Words!

---

1. See explanation in Point II.

Appendix V

THE BANISHING RITUAL OF THE PENTAGRAM

1. Stand, facing East. Use either the index finger of the right hand to trace the lineal figure of the Pentagram, or use a dagger, or a letter-opener shaped like one.

Try to imagine that as you stand, your height increases so that your head is lost in the clouds, while beneath your feet is a small globe, our planet Earth. Then imagine that, as you intone the first line of the ritual, a brilliant light descends from on high.

2. Touch the forehead and vibrate *Atoh* (ah-toh) (Unto Thee, or Thou art.)

3. Imagine the light descending from the forehead, down the body to the feet.

4. Touch the breast (since it would be awkward or ungainly to bend over to touch the feet), and vibrate *Malkuth* (Mahl-kooth) (the Kingdom).

5. Touch the right shoulder with *ve-Gedulah* (and the Glory).

6. Touch the left shoulder with *ve-Geburah* (and the Power).

7. Clasp the hands on the breast, fingers interlaced, saying *le-Olahm Amen* (forever, Amen).

While making gestures 5, 6 and 7, imagine the light crossing from shoulder to shoulder so that actually a large Cross of Light is formed.

8. Turn to East, extend right hand with weapon or index finger, and trace a large Pentagram, vibrating YHVH. (Yod-hay-vahv-hay). Stab it in the centre, and then say:

9. Turn to the South, repeat, but vibrate ADNI (ah-doh-nye).

10. Turn to the West, repeat, but vibrate AHIH (eh-huh-yeh).

11. Turn to the North, repeat, but vibrate AGLA (ah-galah).

(Each Pentagram is to be stabbed in the centre, while vibrating the appropriate Name.)

12. Return to East, touching that point in space, imaginatively, that one started out from in 8.

13. Extend arms in form of a cross, and vibrate:

14. Before me RAPHAEL (rah-phah-ale).

15. Behind me GABRIEL (gah-bree-ale).

16. On my right hand, MICHAEL (mee-chah-ale).

17. On my left hand, AURIEL (awe-ree-ale).

18. For about me flames the Pentagrams,

19. And in the column stands the six-rayed star.

20. Repeat Qabalistic Cross, 1–7.

This may be used primarily for banishing, but may be also employed for invoking the element of Earth. The following are the lineal figures employed.

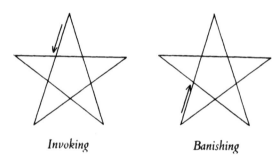

Invoking   *Banishing*

N.B. The cardinal rule is that you move towards the angle involved in order to Invoke. Move away from the angle to Banish.

The Greater Ritual of the Pentagram

The Pentagrams are traced in the air with the sword or other weapon, the name spoken aloud, and the signs used, as illustrated.

All the other appropriate Divine Names will be found in Chapter II, with pronunciation.

The Pentagrams of Spirit.

Equilibrium of Actives
Name: **A H I H** (Eheieh)

  = Spirit symbol.

Equilibrium of Passives
Name: **A G L A** (Agla)

The signs of the Portal: Extend the hands in front of you, palms outwards, separate them as if in the act of rending asunder a veil or curtain (actives), and then bring them together as if closing it up again and let them fall to the side (passives).

(The Grade of the 'Portal' is particularly attributed to the element of Spirit.)

The Pentagrams of Fire.

Name: **A L H I M**
(Elohim).
𝛺 = Fire Kerub

The signs of 4°=7□. Raise the arms above the head and join the hands, so that the tips of the fingers and of the thumbs meet, formulating a triangle (see illustration).

(The Grade of 4°=7□ is particularly attributed to the element Fire.)

The Pentagrams of Water.

Name: A L (El).
⟅≋⟆= Eagle or Water
    Kerub.

The signs of 3°=8□. Raise the arm till the elbows are on a level with the shoulders, bring the hands across the chest, touching the thumbs and tips of fingers so as to form a triangle apex downwards.

(The Grade of 3°=8□ is particularly attributed to the element of Water.)

The Pentagrams of Air.

Name: I H V H (Ye-ho-wau).

♒ = Air Kerub.

The signs of 2°=9□. Stretch both arms upwards and outwards, the elbows bent at right angles, the hand bent back, the palms upwards as if supporting a weight.

(The Grade of 2°=9□ is particularly attributed to the element Air.)

The Pentagrams of Earth.

Name: A D N I (Adonai)

♉ = Earth Kerub.

The Sign of 1°=10□. Advance the right foot, stretch out the right hand upwards and forwards, the left hand downwards and backwards, the palms open.

(The Grade of 1°=10□ is particularly attributed to the element of Earth.)

The Lesser Ritual of the Hexagram

This ritual is to be performed after the 'Lesser Ritual of the Pentagram'.

(I) Stand upright, feet together, left arm at side, right across body, holding Wand or other weapon upright in the median line. Then face East and say:

(II) I.N.R.I.
   Yod, Nun, Resh, Yod.
   Virgo, Isis, Mighty Mother.
   Scorpio, Apophis, Destroyer.
   Sol, Osiris, Slain and Risen.
   Isis, Apophis, Osiris, IA ∩.

(III) Extend the arms in the form of a cross, and say 'The Sign of Osiris Slain.'

(IV) Raise the right arm to point upwards, keeping the elbow square, and lower the left arm to point downwards, keeping the elbow square, and say, 'The Sign of the Mourning of Isis'.

(V) Raise the arms at an angle of sixty degrees to each other above the head, which is thrown back, and say, 'The Sign of Apophis and Typhon'.

(VI) Cross the arms on the breast, and bow the head and say, 'The Sign of Osiris Risen'.

(VII) Extend arms as in (III) and cross them again as in (VI), saying 'L.V.X., Lux, the Light of the Cross'.

(VIII) Trace banishing hexagram of Saturn, vibrating while doing so, ARARITA. Then trace in centre of the figure, ♄ while vibrating YHVH ELOHIM (yuh-hoh-voh ay-loh-heem).

(IX) Repeat same hexagram and names in all four quarters, then returning to the East.

(X) Repeat the Opening gesture to close the Ritual.

The Greater Ritual of the Hexagram utilizes the same principles, but employs the other planetary hexagrams as follows:

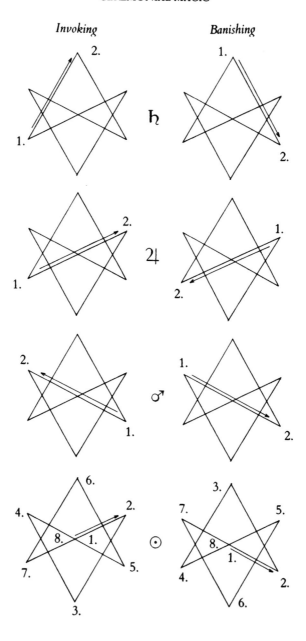

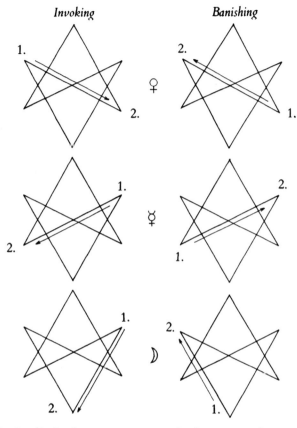

N.B. Cardinal rule is to move towards planetary angle to invoke – away from to banish. Signs of the Zodiac may be dealt with by employing their planetary rulers.

Attributions of the Planets to the Angles of the Hexagram.

FOUNDATIONS OF PRACTICAL MAGIC

An Introduction to Qabalistic, Magical and Meditative Techniques

Israel Regardie. Writings by a famous occultist which collate a lifetime's experience of occult techniques to form an accessible system of practical magic. Explains the three main divisions of magic—divination, evocation and invocation; meditation through mantras, free association, breathing and visualization exercises; gematria and hieroglyphic symbolism, with particular reference to the Hermetic Order of the Golden Dawn.